SpringerBriefs in Psychology

SpringerBriefs in Behavioral Criminology

Series Editor
Vincent B. Van Hasselt, Fort Lauderdale, Florida, USA

Behavioral Criminology is a multidisciplinary approach that draws on behavioral research for the application of behavioral theories and methods to assessment, prevention, and intervention efforts directed toward violent crime and criminal behavior. Disciplines relevant to this field are criminology; criminal justice (law enforcement and corrections); forensic, correctional, and clinical psychology and psychiatry: neuropsychology, neurobiology, conflict and dispute resolution; sociology, and epidemiology. Areas of study and application include, but are not limited to: specific crimes and perpetrators (e.g., homicide and sex crimes, crimes against children, child exploitation, domestic, school, and workplace violence), topics of current national and international interest and concern (e.g., terrorism and counter terrorism, cyber crime), and strategies geared toward evaluation, identification, and interdiction with regard to criminal acts (e.g., hostage negotiation, criminal investigative analysis, threat and risk assessment). The aim of the proposed Briefs is to provide practitioners and researchers with information, data, and current best practices on important and timely topics in Behavioral Criminology. Each Brief will include a review of relevant research in the area, original data, implications of findings, case illustrations (where relevant), and recommendations for directions that future efforts might take.

David M. Feldman • Paul M. Silvasi •
Dayna Rotshtyn • Caleigh Covell

Intersections of the Legal System and the Deaf Community

From Law Enforcement to Incarceration

Springer

David M. Feldman
Nova Southeastern University
Fort Lauderdale, FL, USA

Paul M. Silvasi
Utah State Hospital
Provo, UT, USA

Dayna Rotshtyn
Nova Southeastern University
Fort Lauderdale, FL, USA

Caleigh Covell
Nova Southeastern University
Fort Lauderdale, FL, USA

ISSN 2192-8363 ISSN 2192-8371 (electronic)
SpringerBriefs in Psychology
ISSN 2194-1866 ISSN2194-1874 (electronic)
SpringerBriefs in Behavioral Criminology
ISBN 978-3-031-28099-3 ISBN 978-3-031-28100-6 (eBook)
https://doi.org/10.1007/978-3-031-28100-6

This Springer imprint is published by the registered company Springer Nature Switzerland AG
The registered company address is: Gewerbestrasse 11, 6330 Cham, Switzerland

Contents

Chapter 1
Understanding Deaf Culture, the Deaf Community, and American Sign Language in a Criminal Justice and Legal Context

1.1 Deaf Identity, Models of Deafness, and the Deaf Community

While current reference materials have reviewed the topic of Deaf cultural identity and American Sign Language, few professionals have addressed these subjects in the context of the criminal justice and legal systems. Both culture and language are important factors that could have significant implications for Deaf suspects, defendants, and inmates at various levels of these systems, such as knowledge and awareness of constitutional rights, the ability to defend oneself against accusations, or equal access to mental health treatment or other interventions. The ability of law enforcement officers, attorneys, court officials, and correctional staff to interact with and provide services to Deaf suspects, defendants, or inmates will also be affected by Deaf cultural, and languages aspects. Knowledge and awareness of Deaf culture signed language and communication modalities, and available accommodations will likely determine the effectiveness of the criminal justice and legal systems in their ability to provide equal access to services.

Historically, deaf people have been viewed through a "medical" model (Branson & Miller, 2002), which has been used by the hearing majority to label and describe those who are deaf as simply having some impairment in the ability to hear (Lane et al., 1996; Ladd, 2003). However, more modern views of deafness, used by the Deaf community, are more inclusive and suggest that the word "deaf" can mean many things. It can signify a cultural affiliation, a connection to a community, a personal or group identity, or simply indicate a level of functioning related to the ability to hear. Rather

D. M. Feldman et al., *Intersections of the Legal System and the Deaf Community*, SpringerBriefs in Psychology, https://doi.org/10.1007/978-3-031-28100-6_1

than being "placed" into a category, by a hearing majority, more modern approaches view one's identification with "deafness" as a personal choice which may be based on many factors including parents and family dynamics, peers and socialization, educational setting, or level of comfort. Thus, a much broader spectrum of deafness includes such conceptualizations as hearing adjacent, bicultural, or marginal (Bat-Chava, 2000).

This makes the actual number of deaf people in the United States somewhat difficult to determine as much depends on the researcher's definition of "deaf." Approximately 5% of the general population of the United States has some sort of hearing loss (Woodcock et al., 2007). However, this number includes any degree of hearing loss and does not account for the wide range of variability among deaf people. From a practical standpoint, the etiology and age of deafness may be important and have a significant impact on development and therefore one's self-identification.

The meaning behind "***d***eaf or ***D***eaf" is important to recognize, as the context of the word(s) is descriptive and related to the intent behind which should be used. The choice of the upper or lower casing of the letter "d" will often indicate ability vs. culture and how that deaf person identifies themselves in relation to hearing loss and connection to the Deaf community. There are a number of conventions with regard to whether, or when to, refer to a deaf person, or groups as uppercase "Deaf" or lowercase "deaf" (Napier et al., 2006).

Traditionally, any person with a hearing loss was categorized as deaf (lowercase "d"), which referred only to a pathological condition viewed as requiring correction (speech reading, hearing aids, cochlear implants, etc.). This term, or expression of condition, refers to hearing loss alone and does not necessarily imply a connection to the Deaf community, Deaf culture, or the utilization of a signed language (Padden & Humphries, 1988). Those who choose to identify themselves as "deaf" likely identify more with the "hearing world" as reflected in their choices of communication, assistive technology, and socialization. The term "hearing impaired" would also fall into that category.

A more current and culturally based model recognizes the existence of a much wider spectrum of deafness and the idea of a Deaf culture and Deaf community (Lane et al., 1996). In this context, the term "Deaf," with its capitalized "D," reflects Deafness viewed from a cultural and sociolinguistic framework (Holt et al., 1994). Deaf (capital "D") will generally refer to individuals who identify themselves as "culturally" Deaf and imply a connection to the Deaf community (Padden & Humphries, 1988). Those Deaf individuals who identify as culturally Deaf will likely have a connection to

Deaf culture and the Deaf community and utilize American Sign Language as their primary means of communication. Even within the Deaf community as a whole, there may be variations in the strength, bond, or connection to a Deaf cultural identity and usage or proficiency of ASL. The Deaf community is made up of a diverse group of individuals with a variety of levels of hearing loss yet with similar language preferences and cultural identities. The Deaf community is also a group that varies across socioeconomic status, ethnicity, religion, and many other demographics (Pray & Jordan, 2010). There are specific multicultural and diverse Deaf communities with their own cultural identities, such as Black, Latino, LGBTQ+, and many others (Foss, 2014). Each of these is with both a Deaf identity and a second cultural identity and often with particular nuances of Deaf culture and sign language. The extent to which a person identifies Deaf may range from those whose hearing is only slightly impaired to individuals with profound hearing loss. The onset, type, or level of hearing loss is less important than self-identifying as a culturally Deaf person and participating in the Deaf community (Bat-Chava, 2000).

However, the age of onset of hearing loss may be a factor related to language development, with those who are *prelingually deaf* having differences in terms of communication preferences and proficiency, then those who are *late-deafened*. Prelingual deafness refers to deafness occurring before age 3, where hearing has not, and cannot, be used to learn language, and individuals in this category may have constricted vocabularies and poor English and literacy skills (Vernon & Raifman, 1997). Those who are prelingually Deaf may find learning English to be more challenging as it is a language which they have never heard or spoken in any meaningful way. While ASL proficiency may still be acquired in prelingually Deaf children, just being prelingually deaf does not assure that this will occur. Typically, family, educational, and social interactions are better predictors of ASL development and utilization, but it is not a guarantee of any connection with Deaf culture or community.

The term "late-deafened" refers to those who became deaf after exposure to spoken language and primarily to those who became deaf as adults. Some late-deafened adults may choose to continue to identify as hearing, as this is the more familiar means of socialization and communication, and show no interest in signed communication or the Deaf community. Others may choose to identify as Deaf, learn American Sign Language, and form bonds with Deaf culture and the Deaf community. In some cases, the late-deafened adult may have more proficiency in the English language and struggle with sign language.

1.2 American Sign Language (ASL) and Other Forms of Signed Communication

American Sign Language (ASL) is a complete language that employs signs made with the hands as well as other bodily movements or facial expressions. ASL is based on the idea that sight is the most useful tool a Deaf person has to express and receive communication. It is essential to understand that ASL is distinct and independent from English. There are specific rules of grammar, production, and structure within ASL. Although concepts may be translated from ASL to English, or English to ASL, ASL and English cannot be directly translated word for word. Furthermore, because ASL is a visual language, there is no actual written format (Lane, 1988).

Some signs may be iconic, the shape of the hands representing mimicking the shape or characteristics of the object (e.g., milk, phone, cat), or be more abstract but express a specific concept or idea (e.g., want, thank you, happy). American Sign Language is not just a collection of randomly assigned gestures, and there are strict rules of grammar, production, movement, and "signing space." American Sign Language not only uses signs based on handshapes to convey thoughts and ideas but is also largely reliant on the movements of the shoulders and body and facial expressions to provide context and affect, which in spoken language is manifested in tone, pitch, and volume. In addition to the rules of handshapes, there are specific rules and meanings relating to hand placement, directionality, and movement.

ASL and English are not mutually translatable, and there are major differences between the two languages in terms of grammar, syntax, and presentation (Lane, 1988). English sentence order is *subject-verb-object* ("*I* am *going* to the *store*"), while in ASL, it is *object-subject-verb* ("*store I go*"). Many English words do not have an ASL equivalent (e.g., "charges"). Some words like "right" may be signed in multiple ways and with a different meaning (e.g., "right" as in *directional right turn, a correct response/choice, a legal right, or "it's all right"*). Much depends on one's knowledge and understanding of ASL and the context, or situation of, what is being communicated.

Even within signed communication methods, there are different modalities. There are *signed languages*, such as American Sign Language (ASL), and those utilized in other countries, such as British Sign Language (BSL), Australian Sign Language (AUSLAN), Langue des Signes Québécoise (Quebec Sign Language or LSQ), and Spanish Sign Language (Lengua de Signos Española or LSE). There are also other forms of signed communication styles that exist but are not considered to be actual languages, such as Pidgin Signed English (PSE), Signed Exact English (SEE), and Cued

Speech. However, these are not universally compatible with each other and are independent of ASL.

There are also regional differences in ASL, such as dialects, accents, and cultural variations that may include specific (nonstandard) signs for objects or ideas, signing styles, and the body and facial expressions that serve to accentuate or provide context. For example, "Black Sign Language" is a form of ASL that utilizes a more stylistic approach to signing for many African American Deaf people. If the deaf person is from another country, they may not be familiar with ASL, as their country of origin may use a completely different system. It is very important for the forensic psychologist to recognize that simply providing an ASL interpreter without consideration of these demographic factors will be ineffective if the Deaf defendant does not know or is not proficient in ASL.

It is important to note here that not all deaf people utilize signing in any form as a means of communication and a thorough review and understanding of the deaf suspect, defendants, or inmates' abilities, backgrounds, and preferences for communication must be reviewed and evaluated. There is also a wide range in American Sign Language (ASL) fluency among Deaf people, in the United States, which is often based on such things as age of hearing-loss onset, early access to any language, education, social and family factors, and age at which ASL was first learned. Approximately 90% of deaf children have hearing parents, the majority of whom have either no, or very limited, knowledge of ASL or other signed communication systems (Moreland et al., 2015). The result of this is that in many cases, a deaf child's first form of communication will likely rely on oral/speech/lip reading techniques which may potentially cause language delays in ASL. In addition, as most hearing parents have no personal experience with, or even awareness of, Deaf culture, little opportunity is provided to the deaf child for social interaction or sign language development. Because of this, many deaf individuals are neither fluent in ASL or English, and as a result, the average deaf person reads at a much lower rate than their hearing peers (Holt et al., 1994).

Traditionally outside of Deaf schools and the Deaf community, ASL is rarely used or seen. Few hearing individuals have a mastery of ASL necessary for effective communication, and fewer still are mental health, law enforcement, legal, or correctional professionals with any ASL proficiency. This often will make communication between the Deaf defendant and the criminal justice and legal systems difficult, and there are many documented instances of miscommunication, misdiagnosis, and miscarriages of justice as a result (Maryland v. Barker, 1977; Oregon v. Mason, 1980; Wisconsin v. Hindsley, 2000; Tennessee v. Jenkins, 2002). Deaf suspects, defendants, and inmates have been processed through the legal system without regard for cultural differences, been denied interpreters outright, or been provided with unqualified or inappropriate "interpreters." These situations have led to wrongful arrests and prosecutions, unfair trials, and abuse in correctional settings.

1.3 Historical Perspectives on Deaf People and the Legal System

As deafness can be identified in many ways (e.g., hearing impaired, hard of hearing, deaf, Deaf, etc.), the actual numbers of deaf people currently in the various stages of the criminal justice and legal systems are difficult to assess. Not every encounter with a deaf suspect, defendant, or inmate is the hearing status, language preferences, or cultural identity known or accurately recorded. In some cases, deafness may not be identified at all depending on things such as the level of hearing loss, individual functionality (e.g., verbal responses to question, ability for verbal conversation, etc.), or the apprehensions and preferences of the deaf individual to not disclose their hearing loss, for example, in correctional settings where this could be seen as vulnerability by other inmates. Young et al. (2000) examined the needs of deaf people in the United Kingdom's criminal justice system and noted the difficulty in its ability "to describe adequately this population and to provide an appropriate and targeted response to its needs" (p. 567).

Deaf suspects and defendants must be "afforded the same fundamental fairness as English-speaking defendants" and "the failure to do so deprives Deaf Americans of their life or liberty without the due process guaranteed by the Fifth and Fourteenth Amendments" (Hoopes, 2006, p. 28), the application of these rights is often less than optimal, and in some cases, these rights have even been denied. The criminal justice system was not designed with deaf individuals in mind, and few police officers, attorneys, judges, or correctional staff have any real knowledge of the needs of deaf individuals within their systems. In many cases, the specific needs of the Deaf suspect, defendant, or inmate are not understood, not considered, or just ignored. This will leave the Deaf individual at a significant disadvantage when attempting to interact and make informed decisions while navigating these systems which potentially could result in serious negative consequences including the loss of freedom. Deaf suspects, unable to effectively communicate with law enforcement, may find themselves unable to effectively provide information to police officers or comply with (verbally presented) commands. In addition, culturally appropriate behaviors and attempts at communication on the part of the deaf individual (e.g., touching/tapping to get attention, raising hands to sign, gesturing in the direction of the officer) may be seen as threatening and lead to escalations resulting in additional charges or even physical confrontations. The complexities of the legal system are impossible to comprehend without the benefit of language accessibility and leave the Deaf defendant unprepared, unaware of, or unable to utilize their rights to due process. Deaf inmates unable to communicate with correctional officers or other inmates may find themselves at greater risk of victimization and isolation, or unable to participate in rehabilitation programs.

The recognition of the special circumstances surrounding the Deaf community's interactions with the legal system is not a novel concept. In 1856, an article in the American Journal of Insanity titled "On the Legal Rights and Responsibilities of the Deaf and Dumb" attempted to provide guidance on the needs of Deaf people and the legal system (Peet, 1856). The first part of this article describes the various ways deaf people have been viewed throughout history and makes several references to the theoretical association between hearing ability, language, intelligence, legal rights, and theology. The article goes on the cite several cases involving deaf defendants (the majority in England and France) and the legal decisions rendered in each case. What is striking is that in many of these cases, no real attempts were made to facilitate communication and often decisions by the court were made without any regard for, or input from, the deaf defendant. The article concludes with a declaration of "general principles" for legal professionals when working with the deaf. These include the following:

1. that "a deaf-mute is not necessarily more ignorant…than illiterate persons who are not deaf and dumb" and that "a deaf-mute {who possesses} a dialect of gestures {that} is sufficiently copious and precise may manage his own affairs, make civil contracts…and give evidence in a court of justice",
2. that "proper precautions {should be} taken that the interpreters who accompany him before the [court] are faithful, competent, and disinterested",
3. that "they should be carefully examined to ascertain if they possess the necessary degree of knowledge and intelligent will",
4. "where any doubt exists…teachers of the deaf and dumb should be called in as being more able to appreciate such cases…and usually more expert in conveying pantomime than even the friends of the uneducated mute usually are" (Peet, 1856, p. 169).

While there is certainly much controversy in the above author's use of language, these basic principles are similar to what has been suggested as the ideals and accommodations recommended by modern professionals when working with the Deaf community. First is the recognition that the deaf defendant is not (just by deafness alone) more "ignorant or incapable," than a hearing defendant and that sign language is an appropriate means of communication in legal matters (assuming the deaf defendant uses signed communication). Second is that there must be standards for those providing interpreting services in legal settings. Third is that there is variability in deaf individuals and the "possession" of sufficient legal knowledge is an individual factor in evaluations or legal decision making. Fourth is if there is any question about the deaf individual's knowledge and abilities, then experts (on both Deafness and the legal system) should be utilized to help clarify cultural and language challenges that may be affecting the situation and to provide guidance to the legal profession on relevant language and cultural concerns.

Later, in the early twentieth century, the Bill of Rights was half-heartedly reviewed and applied with respect to the deaf defendants (Sheprow, 1999), but not often enforced, which led to negative outcomes and consequences for many deaf defendants who had little or no understanding of their due process and other rights (Bakke, 2000). In the second half of this century in the case of *Miranda v. Arizona (1966)* and the earlier *Escobedo v. Illinois (1964)* case, courts ruled that suspects were required to be told of their constitutional rights. Upon arrest or trial, many complex legal concepts were not explained to the deaf suspect in any accessible form leaving them at a severe disadvantage in legal protections and decision making. It should also be noted that at this time, there was no legal requirement that a deaf suspect or defendant be provided with any accommodations by law enforcement, attorneys (including their own), or the court. The issue of the Deaf defendant and the need for interpreters in court has also been implied in early legal decisions as part of "due process" and "fair opportunity to defend oneself against the state's accusations" rights (Chambers v. Mississippi, 1973). Vasquez v. State (1991) included the right to "trial proceedings interpreted into a language that a defendant can understand." In addition, there are requirements that a defendant be more than "physically present" and "be informed about the proceedings so he or she can assist in the defense" and that they be provided "a meaningful opportunity to present a complete defense" (State v. Caldron, 2000; Hawkins v. Costello, 2006). While none of these cases are specific to Deaf defendants, they have been applied to deaf suspects and the implication is that equal access to communication is required to ensure a complete defense and a defendant's due process.

More pertinent for Deaf defendants, the Sixth Amendment right to participate in one's own defense has been interpreted to include the right to "accommodations for impairments" and that there exists "the right to have a competent translator assist him…throughout his trial" (United States ex Rel. Negron v. State of N.Y., 1970). In 1978, the Bilingual, Hearing, and Speech-Impaired Court Interpreter Act was adopted by federal court for any civil or criminal action. This required that a qualified interpreter be provided by the court in which a deaf, speech-impaired, or non-English speaking person must participate. Services are paid for by the court when the actions are initiated by the court, but not when the actions are initiated by the Deaf person (BHSICIA, 1978). Currently, the Americans with Disabilities Act (ADA, 1990) identifies deafness as a disability and recognizes impairment in linguistic skills "if (they) do not speak or adequately understand English (or a comparable language) because of deafness" (Dubow & Geer, 1992). As such, "reasonable accommodations" are required to be provided to deaf suspects, defendants, and inmates during various parts of the legal and criminal justice process. Generally, these take the form of sign language interpreters, although other modifications (e.g., assistive technology) may also be provided.

The above is not meant to suggest that the legal system as a whole is in itself intentionally or inherently biased against the deaf community. Rather it is a lack of sufficient awareness and recognition as to the necessary provision of accommodations to meet the needs of the Deaf defendant that is likely at the root of this problem. Law enforcement officers, attorneys, judges, and correctional staff will very likely have no experience or training in the effect that Deaf culture and sign language will have on their various roles and professional activities, duties, and responsibilities. The law enforcement officer arriving at the scene of a crime involving a deaf suspect, the court attempting to render a fair decision regarding a deaf defendant, or the correctional officer tasked with managing a deaf inmate will all be faced with very unique challenges for which they are likely unprepared.

1.4 The Americans with Disabilities Act (ADA), Accommodations, and the Deaf Community

The ADA established the protocol for both private and public entities regarding when a reasonable accommodation must be provided to people with disabilities. The Americans with Disabilities Act (ADA, 1990) identifies deafness as a disability and requires "reasonable accommodations" to be provided to Deaf suspects, defendants, and inmates. Generally, these take the form of sign language interpreters, although other modifications (e.g., assistive technology) may also be provided. The ADA (1990) specifies that the "type of auxiliary aid or service necessary to ensure effective communication will vary in accordance with the method of communication used by the individual; the nature, length, and complexity of the communication involved; and the context in which the communication is taking place." Furthermore, the standard that has been set for effective communication is that a person with a disability should be afforded a level of communication that is substantially equal to that afforded to a nondisabled person (Silvasi, 2020).

However, the much of the wording of the ADA allows for "flexible interpretation." Although it states that "reasonable" accommodations must be provided, it allows some debate on the part of the providing agency to determine what constitutes a "reasonable" accommodation. As the wording is vague, this may limit the deaf person's comprehension, and therefore, right to determine their own needs for accommodations. In many cases, this determination will be made by a non-deaf individual who may not fully understand the needs of the deaf person or the importance of the accommodation. Often accommodations are considered in terms of cost as opposed to usefulness or importance to the deaf person needing the service.

Accommodations are provisions that assist an individual in being more able to *fully* participate in such things as educational, medical, legal, and social activities and situations. They are generally intended to provide aid to a specific function or setting in which they are used. That is, accommodations are supposed to be neutral and transparent. This may include accommodations such as guide dogs and wheelchairs that are viewed as extensions of the individuals who use them in a variety of settings and environments. American Sign Language interpreters are also considered to be an extension of the individual and are there to facilitate the communication between a person who is deaf and the hearing person (or persons).

1.5 The Qualified ASL Interpreter in Forensic Settings

Given the intricacy involved with ASL and English translation, a qualified interpreter is essential to facilitate accurate communication. At this time, there are no established state, or federal, licensure requirements for professional interpreters. However, criteria for certification as an ASL interpreter have been established by the National Registry of Interpreters for the Deaf

(RID) and the Conference of Interpreter Trainers (CIT). A qualified interpreter is an individual who has obtained a national certification from the Registry of Interpreters for the Deaf (RID).

Most Interpreter Training Programs (ITP) in the United States are 2-year Associate Degree programs with some being 4-year bachelor's degree programs. This certification includes training not only in American Sign Language and translation but also in the RID Code of Ethics (RID, 2005). This ethical code for professional interpreters includes such things as rules related to interpreter/client confidentiality, professional conduct, and skills and knowledge guidelines. A qualified interpreter for a legal assignment is able to "interpret effectively, accurately, and impartially, both receptively and expressively, using specialized vocabulary required in a legal setting" (ADA, 1990). The Registry of Interpreters has produced a standard practice paper for legal interpreting (RID, 2005).

Ultimately, the role of the interpreter is to facilitate communication, not to clarify misunderstandings, contribute to the conversation, or provide training to hearing professionals on ASL (Olsen & Kermit, 2014). The utilization of an interpreter alone is not a guarantee to equal access for the person who is Deaf (LaVigne & Vernon, 2003; Olsen & Kermit, 2014), and other factors must be considered relating to individual demographics of each individual. In optimal circumstances, the client should be informed that they will be provided an interpreter and be permitted to have input regarding the type of interpreter or accommodation that they prefer.

Not every hearing person who "can sign" is a qualified interpreter and hearing people who have Deaf family, or have taken ASL classes, may not be proficient or knowledgeable enough to serve in this role. Likewise, there are many deaf individuals who do not sign or use a different form of signed communication (Vernon & Andrews, 2011). Similarly, writing notes in English to Deaf individuals does not equal the services of a qualified interpreter (Miller & Vernon, 2002).

It is important to recognize that "interpreting English into ASL and vice versa requires a great deal of skill" and that "relying on amateurs who know some sign language is a frequent error" (Dubow et al., 1986, p. 2). Family members, friends, attorneys, law enforcement officers, and other "invested" individuals should as a rule, and except in emergency situations, never be used in legal settings even when requested by the Deaf suspect, defendant, or inmate. An example of this situation where the Deaf individual may be a victim of domestic violence, and the interpreter may be the abuser. In addition, there may be times when information needs to be kept private such as sensitive personal information or information regarding financial issues from which a family member/interpreter may benefit.

As with spoken language interpreters, video interpretation is available for sign language interpreters. Video remote interpretations are usually acceptable in situations in which the connection is adequate, and the image does not lag (ADA, 1990). In addition, video remote interpreting is best when it is a one-to-one conversation in an office environment, where the camera can view both the Deaf person's face and hands and the Deaf person can see the interpreter clearly. Video relay loses its effectiveness when you have more than one speaker or signer, when there is movement that the camera does not follow, or the situation is emotional or extremely important.

1.6 The Certified Deaf Interpreters (CDI)

In some cases, a more specialized form of intermediary interpreter must be utilized, known as a Certified Deaf Interpreter (CDI) who attempts to facilitate communication between the deaf individual and the ASL interpreter (who then facilitates communication with the hearing forensic psychologist). CDIs are Deaf individuals, often children of Deaf parents, who have grown up with ASL and have been certified by the Registry of Interpreters of the Deaf as a result of specialized courses. These "deaf interpreters" have special linguistic skills in ASL idioms and usages used by Deaf people who have very limited ASL skills. The utilization of a CDI is a method that can be used to aid in providing full access to communication in legal situations and proceedings involving nonlinguistic or minimally linguistic Deaf defendants. CDIs work in conjunction with an ASL interpreter and serve as a form of liaison between the ASL interpreter and the hearing professional who is conducting an interview, questioning, or evaluation (Vernon & Andrews, 2011).

Some individuals who are Deaf may have educational, cultural, or additional disability deficits that affect their ability to understand American Sign Language. There are also the Deaf individuals who use or rely on "home" or more culturally based, signs that are utilized within families, or as part of a cultural minority group, and their preferred signs may not be standard ASL. For these Deaf defendants who may not be fluent in any sign language, a Certified Deaf Interpreter (CDI) may be needed to facilitate optimal communication. The need for a CDI can often be determined by the ASL interpreter and criminal justice or legal professional working together through interviews with, and review of historical information of, Deaf individual.

1.7 The Utilization of ASL Interpreters in Forensic Settings

Deaf individuals at all levels of the criminal justice system have legal rights that include the ability to take part in any of their proceedings Otherwise, the Deaf suspect, defendant, or inmate is essentially being denied their rights to due process (Vernon & Miller, 2001). Deaf suspects and defendants must be "afforded the same fundamental fairness as English-speaking defendants" and "the failure to do so deprives Deaf Americans of their life or liberty without the due process guaranteed by the Fifth and Fourteenth Amendments" (Hoopes, 2006, p. 28). Absent or incomplete communication can lead to serious consequences for deaf individuals involved in the criminal justice and legal systems. It can deprive them of fully understanding their due process and other rights under the law and constitution. It can also severely limit their ability to communicate with mental health professionals, law enforcement officials, attorneys, correctional officers, or the court (as a witness or defendant).

A qualified interpreter will have and utilize their set of skills to facilitate communication and ensure that the Deaf person's right to participate is not overlooked. Therefore, it is important to use an ASL interpreter who will be familiar with both legal terminology and procedures. This will help ensure that the Deaf suspect, defendant, or inmate can follow and understand the situations related to their arrest, charges, questioning, proceedings, and incarceration. That they will be able to follow conversations, ask questions, and make statements to law enforcement officers, attorneys, judges, and correctional staff. The qualified ASL interpreter can help ensure that the Deaf defendant is understanding their rights and the situation and not at a disadvantage. Interpreting in legal situations is not only limited to law enforcement interactions, court proceedings, and correctional settings, but is also important in such legal situations as attorney/client conferences, depositions, witness interviews, real estate settlements, and contract negotiations. An added layer of complexity arises when considering that interpreters by themselves are not a guarantee to equal access for the deaf suspect, defendant, or inmate (LaVigne & Vernon, 2003; Olsen & Kermit, 2014). Providing an ASL interpreter to a deaf suspect, defendant, or inmate will not be effective if that deaf individual does not know, or is not proficient in, ASL.

Some deaf people prefer an English-based signed system. This system is visual, like American Sign Language, but follows the grammatical rules of spoken English. Other deaf people may rely on the services of an oral interpreter and lip reading. In this scenario, the oral interpreter mouths, without sound, each word to the deaf person (Stewart et al., 1998). Still, others prefer to rely on real-time captioning (Humphries & Alcorn, 1994). This method is similar to the closed caption text at the bottom of a television screen. A captioning machine and laptop are the most common devices used in small settings. The real-time captioner types everything that is said, which appears on the screen of the laptop, and the deaf person reads it. Each of these systems requires and presupposes that the deaf person has fluency in English.

It is highly recommended that law enforcement agencies, courts, and correctional facilities become familiar with interpreter certifications and specialties and the reasons why it is so crucial to make sure that any interpreter obtained and provided meets these standards. The pitfalls of using a noncertified interpreter could be severe in terms of quality of the communication, privacy and privileged communications, and ensuring that communication is unbiased and as fully accessible as possible.

1.8 Conclusion

The Deaf suspect, defendant, or inmates' ability to successfully navigate the legal systems will likely be affected by their "d/Deaf" cultural identity, their language preference, their communication ability, and their connection to the Deaf community. Law enforcement officers, attorneys, judges, correctional staff, and mental health professionals working in the legal system should become aware of the different aspects of hearing loss, language and communication preferences, and cultural identities that may affect the due process rights of deaf individuals within these systems. Failure to be mindful of the needs of the deaf suspect, defendant, or inmate is likely to result in misunderstandings, misdiagnosis, unfair legal outcomes, ineffective treatment, and even danger to the Deaf individual. This ultimately means that the Deaf individual is at a higher risk of having their rights violated at every juncture of the criminal justice and legal process than their hearing counterparts. Mental health, law enforcement, and legal professionals may be the initial advocates for cultural and linguistic awareness and to ensure the accommodations that are required for equal access to services, communication, and due process rights are provided.

References

Americans with Disabilities Act of 1990, Pub. L. No. 101–336, 104 Stat. 328 (1990), § 35.160.

Bakke, D. (2000). *God knows his name: The true story of john doe no. 24*. Southern Illinois University Press.

Bat-Chava, Y. (2000). Diversity of deaf identities. *American Annals of the Deaf, 145*(5), 420–428.

BHSICIA (1978). H.R. 12003 — 95th Congress: Bilingual, Hearing and Speech Impaired Court Interpreter Act. www.GovTrack.us. April 1, 2023.

Branson, J., & Miller, D. (2002). *Damned for their difference: The cultural construction of deaf people as "Disabled": A sociological history*. Washington DC: Gallaudet University Press.

Dubow, S., & Geer, S. (1992). *Legal rights: The guide for deaf and hard of hearing people* (pp. 15–45). Gallaudet University Press.

Dubow, S., Goldberg, L., Geer, S., Gardner, F., Penn, A., Conlon, S., & Charmatz, M. (1986). *Legal rights of hearing impaired persons* (3rd ed., p. 2). Galladuet University Press.

Foss, K. A. (2014). Constructing hearing loss or "deaf gain?" voice, agency, and identity in television's representations of d/deafness. *Critical Studies in Media Communication, 31*(5), 426–447.

Holt, J. A., Hotto, S., & Cole, K. (1994). *Demographic aspects of hearing impairment: Questions and answers* (Center for Assessment & Demographic Studies). Gallaudet University.

Hoopes, R. (2006). Trampling Miranda: Interrogating deaf suspects. In C. Lucas (Ed.), *Language and the law in deaf communities*. Washington, DC: Gallaudet University Press.

Humphrey, J. A., & Alcorn, B. J. (1994). *So you want to be an interpreter? An introduction to sign language interpreting*. Amarillo, TX: H & H Publishers.

Ladd, P. (2003). *Understanding deaf culture: In search of deafhood*. Multilingual Matters.

Lane, H. (1988). Is there a "psychology of the deaf"? *Exceptional Children, 55*(1), 7–19. https://doi.org/10.1177/001440298805500101

Lane, H., Hoffmeister, R., & Bahan, B. (1996). *A journey into the deaf world*. Dawn Sign Press.

LaVigne, M., & Vernon, M. C. (2003). An interpreter isn't enough: Deafness, language, and due process. *Wisconsin Law Review, 5*, 844–936.

Miller, K., & Vernon, M. (2002). Linguistic diversity in deaf defendants and due process rights. *Journal of Deaf Studies and Education, 6*(3), 99. Oxford University Press.

Moreland, C., Atcherson, S. R., Zazove, P., & McKee, M. M. (2015, July). Hearing loss: Issues in the deaf and hard of hearing communities. *FP Essent, 434*, 29–40. PMID: 26161526.

Napier, J., McKee, R. L., & Goswell, D. (2006). *Sign language interpreting: Theory and practice in Australia and New Zealand*. Federation Press.

National Registry of Interpreters for the Deaf (RID). (2005). *Code of ethics*. Silver Spring, MD.

Olsen, T., & Kermit, P. (2014). Sign language, translation, and rule of law – Deaf peoples experiences from encounters with the Norwegian criminal justice system. *Scandinavian Journal of Disability Research, 17*(Sup1), 23–41.

Padden, C., & Humphries, T. (1988). *Deaf in America voices from a culture*. Harvard University Press.

Peet, H. P. (1856). *On the legal rights and responsibilities of the deaf and dumb* (Vol. XII, No. 2). American Journal of Insanity.

Pray, J. L., & Jordan, I. K. (2010). The deaf community and culture at a crossroads: Issues and challenges. *Journal of Social Work in Disability & Rehabilitation, 9*(2), 168–193.

Sheprow, G. J. (1999, December 10). *Interpreting the miranda warnings*. American Sign Language Resources.

Silvasi, P. M. (2020). *Warnings that fell on deaf ears: A three-pronged analysis of encounters between deaf individuals and law enforcement*. Gallaudet University.

Vernon, M., & Raifman, L. (1997). Recognizing and handling problems of incompetent deaf defendants charged with serious crimes. *International Journal of Law and Psychiatry, 20*(3), 373–387.

Vernon, M., & Miller, K. (2001). Linguistic incompetence to stand trial: A unique condition in some deaf defendants. *Journal of Interpreting, Millennial Edition*, 99–120.

Vernon, M., & Andrews, J. (2011). *Basic legal issues in handling cases of defendants who are deaf*. The Champion. National Association of Criminal Defense Lawyers.

Woodcock, K., Rohan, M. J., & Campbell, L. (2007). Equitable representation of deaf people in mainstream academia: Why not? *Higher Education, 53*(3), 359–379.

Young, A., Monteiro, B., & Ridgeway, S. (2000). Deaf people with mental health needs in the criminal justice system: A review of the UK literature. *The Journal of Forensic Psychiatry, 11*(3), 567. Routledge.

Chapter 2
The Deaf Community and Law Enforcement

2.1 Interactions Between Law Enforcement and the Deaf Community

Research on interactions between law enforcement and Deaf community or Deaf suspects is scarce, although some attempts have been made to better analyze and better understand the nature and consequences of such interactions (Garner, 2019) as well as other first responders (Engelman et al., 2013). It has been noted that both Deaf suspects and victims "face significant barriers in their interactions with the police" and that "these barriers can have a detrimental effect not only on deaf individuals, but also in law enforcement efforts to prosecute cases" (McAnnany & Kothekar, 2011, p. 878). Sadly, many examples of cultural and linguistic misunderstandings resulting in the abuse of deaf suspects can be found through searches of the United States Department of Justice (2022), the American Civil Liberties Union (ACLU, 2023), and various media and disability advocacy groups (Smith, 2010; Lewis, 2014; Hsu, 2017).

Existing law enforcement and first responder trainings on recognizing disabilities and understanding the needs of people with disabilities are rare (Nelson, 2012). Typically, when these types of training are available, they are not focused specifically on the challenges faced by the Deaf community but rather a general introduction to the subject. However, some law enforcement agencies have offered, and continue to offer, specific training on interacting with the Deaf suspects and the Deaf community to both their training classes and current officers. Training has also been provided at law schools and attorneys' offices on the Deaf community and legal rights. While

D. M. Feldman et al., *Intersections of the Legal System and the Deaf Community*, SpringerBriefs in Psychology, https://doi.org/10.1007/978-3-031-28100-6_2

sporadic, these training have been met with some enthusiasm and appear to demonstrate at least some interest in and awareness of the potential challenges related to the interactions with Deaf suspects, witnesses, defendants, and victims. There is even a study from the United Kingdom which indicated that law enforcement officers recognize their lack of knowledge of the Deaf community and have identified this as a need for training (Wakeland et al., 2019). In addition, community training for the Deaf community related to interactions with the law enforcement would likely be beneficial. These would serve to (1) develop awareness regarding the rationale for police actions and policies, (2) inform the Deaf community of their due process rights during arrest and questioning, and (3) inform the Deaf community of how to ask for and make clear their communication needs and other accommodation preferences to law enforcement prior to arrest and questioning.

In most cases, the first interaction between a Deaf individual and law enforcement will occur when an officer has either observed some infraction (e.g., traffic violation) or is called to investigate a reported or alleged crime. It is important to note that deafness is a not visible condition and law enforcement officers may not be aware that a suspect is deaf until attempts at communication are made. Visual cues of hearing loss, such as hearing aids or cochlear implants, may not be seen or identified, and communication challenges or preferences will not be immediately known. Even when signed communication is observed, it may readily be identified as such by the officer and instead be seen as noncompliant or threatening act (e.g., aggressive gestures, gang signs). While the decision to file charges is at the discretion of the office of the district or state's attorney, what transpires initially with law enforcement can mitigate or increase accusations and charges. Depending on the specifics of the allegations and the subsequent interactions between the officer and the Deaf suspect, this will be the first step in a process that may include questioning, criminal prosecution, court appearances, incarceration, or other legally determined punitive actions.

For many individuals who are Deaf, the initial contact with law enforcement officers is likely to be confusing, challenging, and even frightening due to language barriers and lack of access to information. For the Deaf suspect, the outcome of such interactions will likely be highly dependent on effective communication and cultural awareness that not be known to or recognized by most law enforcement officers. Important and consequential information will need to be communicated to the Deaf suspect, and the Deaf suspect will need to communicate information back to the officer. Miscommunications and misunderstandings can occur at any of the various points of officer contact beginning with the arrival on scene and continuing through arrest,

Miranda warnings, and questioning. At each of these stages, effective communication is essential to provide the Deaf suspect with instructions, information, and their rights. In addition, the Deaf suspect should be provided with the opportunity to ask questions and provide details related to the situation. Depending on the skills and ability of the officer and the Deaf suspect to communicate effectively, misunderstandings may occur and the consequences for such misunderstandings could easily escalate the situations and result in arrest, additional charges, or physical altercations.

2.2 Interactions with Law Enforcement and the Deaf Community

The majority of law enforcement officers are well trained in department policy and procedural regulations. They are adept at following a specific set of rules that govern their actions in the community and for safety of themselves, citizens, and suspects. While this may be efficient for the more the average hearing individual encountered during a routine day, it will likely be much more challenging for situations involving a deaf individual. Police training will dictate that, in certain situations, the officer stands in specific places. It also informs how an officer will approach a situation, when they can lawfully apply restraints, or what may justify physical contact. All of these procedures make sense from a policing perspective and are intended to ensure the safety of the officer, the suspect, and the public. None of those procedures impede communication between a police officer and a hearing suspect. However, they can be extremely challenging for a Deaf suspect when communication is cut off and there appears to be no way to effectively interact with the officer.

Few police officers possess any knowledge of Deaf culture or the Deaf community, and fewer still have any proficiency in sign language communication. This means that there will be little to no efficient direct communication between the Deaf suspect and the officer. Even officers that may have a rudimental knowledge of sign language will not likely be able to utilize this skill in an efficient enough manner to allow for meaningful communication of such complex and consequential information. Typically, in the initial interactions between the officer and the deaf individual, attempts are made using inefficient communication methods such as lip reading, note passing, gesture, or fingerspelling. Law enforcement officers should be cautioned about overestimating their ability to *effectively* communicate using any of these methods.

When Deaf suspects attempt to use sign language in order to communicate, these may be interpreted as a threat, resistance, or behavior that indicates mental disturbance. Perceiving these attempts at sign language in this way, law enforcement officers may attempt to physically restrain, or handcuff, the Deaf suspect, which in turn may lead to more frantic signing or gesturing viewed as "resistance" resulting in additional use of force and possibly additional charges (Scharper, 2009). Deaf suspects attempt to adjust their position to better see the officer may be viewed as noncompliant, resistant, or aggressive, especially if the Deaf suspect did not hear a command to stay in place. In at least one case, a Deaf suspect's sign language attempts were mistakenly viewed by police as "flashing gang signs" (Herman, 1997). Deaf suspects will not be aware of officer's presence if approaching from behind and will have essentially cut off communication if standing behind the Deaf suspect (Sandlin, 1995). Not following instructions may initially be viewed as noncompliance as opposed to the Deaf suspects' inability to hear the commands (Lewis v. Truitt, 1997). When hands are restrained, in front of or behind the back, the Deaf suspect has lost the ability to communicate through signs and may struggle in ways which appear to be threatening and resisting arrest. The inability to hear, and therefore respond, to commands made by officers has been noted in many instances where Deaf suspects and law enforcement have crossed paths resulting negative outcomes for the Deaf suspect (Andone, 2017; Herman, 1997).

In some states or jurisdictions, place cards, or indicators on a driver's license, which help to identify the individual as Deaf and are available from motor vehicle departments or other government agencies. Place cards can be left in the driver's side back window or kept in glove or arm-rest compartment, or a window shade, to be used as needed. While this may seem like a viable solution for both the Deaf community and law enforcement, it is not without challenges. Some Deaf individuals have expressed concern that the place cards, if left in the window, identify them as Deaf and make them more likely to become a victim of a crime. Others have expressed concern that leaving the card in the window or indicating "deaf" on a driver's license makes their private and personal information public and possibly subject to discrimination. The keeping of place cards in the glove or armrest compartment also raises concerns as when stopped as Deaf driver will be seen by the officer as reaching for "something" and not remaining still when ordered to do so. The impression they are reaching for a weapon and not following commands to stop will in all likelihood escalate the situation and possibly result in a deadly, reaction from the officer who mistakenly feels their safety to be in jeopardy (Twersky-Glasner, 2006, Herman, 1997).

2.3 Deaf Suspects and Police Interrogations: The Challenges of Administering the Miranda Warnings

Under the justice system of the United States, all suspects are entitled to a Miranda warning at the time of arrest, which outlines the rights and considerations afforded to the arrestee, such as the right to an attorney and the right not to incriminate oneself (Miranda v. Arizona, 1966). This critical piece of the due process provides protection to the suspect and allows them to be informed of the potential consequences of their choices or actions. As such, Deaf suspects and defendants must be "afforded the same fundamental fairness as English-speaking defendants" and "the failure to do so deprives Deaf Americans of their life or liberty without the due process guaranteed by the Fifth and Fourteenth Amendments" (Hoopes, 2006a, b, pp. 26, 28). Historically, due to linguistic, reading, and educational challenges, the Miranda warning when given to Deaf suspect has rarely been presented in a manner that meets with this ideal (Andrews et al., 2007). In such cases, it is more likely to be done in a way the Deaf suspect cannot fully comprehend and, therefore, they are not made truly aware of their rights. Studies of the comprehension of the Miranda warnings and Deaf suspects have found that approximately 30% "are not properly informed of their privilege against self-incrimination and their right to an attorney" (Anon, 1992a, b). Therefore, much caution and consideration should be observed with Deaf suspects in the administration of the Miranda warnings and any subsequent questioning, interviews, or interrogations. There are many examples of the negative consequences resulting from inappropriately administered Miranda warnings by the police (Maryland v. Barker, 1977; Oregon v. Mason, 1980; Wisconsin v. Hindsley, 2000; Tennessee v. Jenkins, 2002).

There are "three possibilities" for the presentation of the Miranda warnings to the Deaf suspect available to law enforcement (Vernon et al., 1996c, p. 122), although each presents with specific challenges and no one method is necessarily the best for all Deaf suspects, considering the variety of cultural and linguistic differences within the Deaf community as a whole.

The first option is for the officer to present the warnings to the Deaf suspect verbally, as they would to any other suspect. However, this presumes that the Deaf suspect is able to read their speech/lips well enough to be considered effective communication and that they will be able to comprehend the meanings behind the warnings and be enabled to make an informed choice. This is typically not considered a satisfactory solution, and the likelihood of any Deaf suspect fully understanding the meaning and intent of the warnings is remote. For example, it has been found that "of the 42 phonemes that make up the sound of the English language half look like some other sound as formed on the lips or else are invisible" (Davis & Hardick, 1981, pp. 59–60). Eckhardt & Anastas (2007) noted that "on average the deaf adult will not understand more than 26%–40% of one-on-one conversation through lip-reading" (p. 241), and the United States Department of Justice (2006) has also noted that "only about one third of spoken words can be understood by speech reading." Clearly, administration of the Miranda warnings in this format is grossly insufficient for Deaf suspects, especially those who prefer sign language. However, it is important to note that some deaf people have been raised "orally" and do not utilize any form of signed communication. These deaf individuals may have a preference for an oral administration, and methods which involve signing may actually be less efficient in this circumstance. As always, care, caution, and consideration should be applied in determining communication preferences, and there should be input from the Deaf suspect as to their needs.

A second option is to administer a written format of the Miranda warnings for the Deaf suspect to read, typically on a note card. The ability to read and comprehend written English varies greatly among people who are Deaf and is dependent on such things as level of education, language development, education, and social exposure. Vernon (1996a) noted that a reading level of eighth grade or higher is required for the "acceptable" comprehension of the Miranda warnings in printed form (p. 123). Most Deaf individuals read at approximately the fifth-grade level (Easterbrooks & Beal-Alvarez, 2012), and data suggests that approximately 60% of Deaf individuals do not read well enough to comprehend the information provided in the Miranda warnings (Anon, 1992a, b). Therefore, simply having the Deaf suspect read the warnings off a card will not likely be possible with the majority of Deaf suspects and certainly not enough for the Deaf suspect to fully comprehend what they are reading so that the warnings have any real value. As it is not possible for an arresting officer, an attorney, or an interpreter to know with certainty the reading level of the Deaf suspect from general interactions or conversation, extreme caution in assuming the Deaf suspect's reading ability is recommended. Furthermore, without some form of empirically validated measure of reading, it will likely be impossible to determine reading level accurately. In most cases involving defendants who are Deaf, it is the defense attorney who will be responsible for ensuring if the Miranda warnings were administered in a way that assures that the deaf suspect was fully aware of his rights (Sheprow, 1999).

The third option would be to sign the Miranda warnings, and of the three, this may be the best method in circumstances with a signing Deaf suspect. However, there is still a myriad of problems associated with using sign language for such a complex task, and it is by no means a perfect solution for all signing Deaf suspects. First, this method assumes that the Deaf suspect utilizes and has proficiency in some form of sign language as their primary means of communication, and this would need to be determined prior to the administration of the warnings. An interpreter signing, in any form, to a Deaf suspect who does use sign language would be of little or no value. As noted in the previous chapter, there are many different types of communication modalities currently in use, and an interpreter signing to a Deaf suspect in ASL when that suspect uses Cued Speech would also not likely provide any measurable understanding of the warnings. To further complicate matters, ASL and English are not mutually translatable, and there are major differences between the two languages. Therefore, a word-for-word translation would likely be confusing and not representative of the intent behind the warnings. There are also many legal terms for which there are no signs, or the signs are only known to better-educated deaf people possessing legal or academic backgrounds (Vernon, 1996a). Simply finger spelling the Miranda warnings (e.g., manual alphabet) is also not an accurate, or time-efficient, means of signed presentation to Deaf suspects. First, if the warnings are spelled to an illiterate or poorly educated Deaf person, they will not be understood (Dubow & Greer, 1992). Second, expressive and receptive fingerspelling would likely be exhausting for both the signer and the Deaf suspect. If the Deaf suspect has expressed a preference for sign language and requested a sign language interpreter, any Miranda administration or questioning should be put on hold until the language and communication issues are resolved, and the requested interpreter arrives (Vernon et al., 2001). However, sign language does appear to be the most effective method for the communication of the Miranda warnings, although there are several factors to consider:

1. Is sign language the preferred means of communication for the Deaf suspect? And, if so, what kind of sign language or communication is used?
2. Is the level of proficiency in that language possessed by the deaf suspect to the extent that the warnings will be meaningful?
3. Does the interpreter have prerequisite qualifications and skills to present the warnings in a way that can be fully comprehended by the deaf suspect?

    (a) Are specialist interpreters, such as the CDI, needed?

The optimal situation is a Deaf suspect that is fluent in ASL and provided with a skilled ASL interpreter familiar with the intent behind the Miranda warnings. However, this may not be a frequently occurring combination and various Deaf individuals have different signing abilities, and various interpreters have different skills related to specific types of interpreting settings and situations.

The US Department of Justice, Office of Justice Programs, has a video which aims to "inform police officers about the approaches that should and should not be used in the presentation of the Miranda warnings prior to the questioning of deaf persons who are in police custody" (USDOJ, 2019). This video dramatizes several methods of administering the Miranda warnings and notes "inadequacies" of administration through lip-reading ability, written copy, and even through the use of a sign language interpreter. The video goes on to advise that the police should "not even attempt" to administer the warnings until the suspects' attorney is present and that all meetings between police, attorneys, and the deaf suspect should be videotaped (USDOJ, 2019). Vernon (1996b) has also developed a template of the Miranda warnings administration that he has suggested for use with deaf suspects (p. 128). Several states (Oklahoma, 2007; Tennessee, 2010; Arizona, 2003) have all enacted requirements that a sign language interpreter be provided prior to a statement being taken and recognizing the need for an interpreter that best fits the needs of the suspect.

The USDOJ also regulates the provision of interpreters for police departments receiving federal funding. Among other things, these regulations specifically state: "law enforcement agencies should provide for qualified interpreters to assist agencies when dealing with hearing-impaired persons"; and that "it is the responsibility of the law enforcement agency to determine uses ASL or signed English to communicate"; and "the law enforcement agency has an obligation under federal law to offer an interpreter to the arrestee with no cost" (USDOJ, 2020, p. 503). Furthermore, "complainants and victims are also entitled to have interpreters" (McEntee, 1995, p. 186).

It is not practical to expect all, or even some, law enforcement officers to become proficient enough in ASL for any meaningful or effective communication. In fact, it is not recommended that law enforcement officers use anything but the most basic signs or gestures and to use them only in emergency or life-threatening situations. Even the law enforcement officers' assumptions that because the suspect is deaf that they therefore must use ASL can be a huge, and costly, mistake. Unless the law enforcement officer has some documented proficiency in ASL, attempting to communicate complex and legal information in this way is not advised.

As noted previously, few opportunities for training on successful interactions with the Deaf community are provided, leaving officers often unaware of need for, and how to acquire, an interpreter or of any department policy or process for doing so. It is important that law enforcement agencies and individual law enforcement officers are familiar with the reasons for an interpreter, when to provide one, and the process by which they can acquire an interpreter prior to potential interactions with Deaf suspects. For this reason, law enforcement training in community relations with the Deaf community and department policies on the utilization of, and provision of, interpreters, or other accommodations, is recommended. When possible, it may be helpful for a single officer to be designated as a form of liaison between the department, the Deaf community, and the interpreting agency to ensure the appropriate accommodations are requested and in place as quickly as possible. It is also suggested that law enforcement agencies build relationships with interpreting agencies, Deaf Service Centers, and the Deaf Community who can provide training and consultation.

2.4 Conclusion

As noted in this chapter, there is a myriad of ways in which interactions between law enforcement officers and Deaf suspects can be challenging. Statements obtained from Deaf suspects who were improperly administered the Miranda warnings would likely be inadmissible in court. Miscommunications and misunderstandings could result in escalations and possibly physical confrontations, and, lastly, improper or unprovided accommodations could result in serious negative consequences for the Deaf suspect and lead to a lack of trust and cooperation with law enforcement by the Deaf community. To avoid these difficulties, agencies and officers should strive to increase their cultural awareness when it comes to the Deaf community and to effectively accommodate communication needs. It has been suggested that this would increase the effectiveness of police interactions with Deaf suspects, and the trust of the Deaf community in their local law enforcement agency. In his study, Silvasi (2020) found that misunderstandings and miscommunications contribute to a highly stressful situation for both police officers and Deaf citizens. In his application of the deference exchange theory (Bonner, 2015) to his findings, Silvasi concluded that when an officer gives a command, and it is not received by the Deaf individual, it is perplexing and confusing for the officer and can escalate the situation if they do not have the appropriate cultural sensitivity to recognize and adapt to these events. Additionally, it was found that Deaf participants who indicated that they felt more at ease during their interaction with law enforcement also acknowledged that the officer accommodated their communication needs. This is similar to findings made by Hajek et al. (2008), who found that communication accommodations from the police resulted in more citizen trust in the police and predicted positive attitudes about complying with police requests.

References

American Civil Liberties Union (ACLU). (2023). Retrieved from https://www.aclu.org/

Andone, D. (2017, September 21). 'He can't hear you': Officers shoot, kill deaf man after giving verbal orders. *CNN*. Accessed at https://www.cnn.com/2017/09/21/us/police-shoot-deaf-man-oklahoma-citytrnd/index.htm

Andrews, J. F., Vernon, M., & LaVigne, M. (2007). The Bill of Rights, due process and the deaf suspect. *Journal of Interpreting, 2007*, 9–38.

Anon, L. (1992a). *Annual survey of deaf and hard of hearing children and youth*. Gallaudet University Press.

Anon, L. (1992b). *Deaf suspects and the Miranda warnings (Video)*. Police Executive Research Forum.

ARIZ. REV. STAT. ANN. § 12-242(C) (2003).

Bonner, H. S. (2015). Police officer decision-making in dispute encounters: Digging deeper into the 'black box'. *American Journal of Criminal Justice, 40*(3), 493–522.

Davis, J. M., & Hardick, E. J. (1981). *Rehabilitation audiology for children and youth*. Wiley.

Dubow, S., & Greer, S. (1992). *Legal rights: The guide for deaf and hard of hearing people*. Gallaudet University Press.

Easterbrooks, S. R., & Beal-Alvarez, J. S. (2012). States' reading outcomes of students who are d/deaf and hard of hearing. *American Annals of the Deaf, 157*(1), 27–40. http://www.jstor.org/stable/26235186

Eckhardt, E., & Anastas, J. (2007). Research methods with disabled populations. *Journal of Social Work in Disability & Rehabilitation, 6*, 233–249.

Engelman, A., Ilvey, S., Tseng, W., Dahrogue, D., Brune, J., & Neurhauser, L. (2013). Responding to the deaf in disasters: Establishing a need for systematic training for state-level emergency management agencies and community organizations. *BMC Health Services Research, 13*, 84. https://doi.org/10.1186/1472-6963-13-84

Garner, J. (2019). *The deaf & law enforcement listening though deaf eyes: A grounded theory approach*. Doctoral dissertation. Nova Southeastern University. Retrieved from NSUWorks, Abraham S. Fischler College of Education. (228). https://nsuworks.nova.edu/fse_etd/228

Hajek, C., Giles, H., Barker, V., Lin, M. C., Zhang, Y. B., & Lee Hummert, M. (2008). Expressed trust and compliance in police-civilian encounters: The role of communication accommodation in Chinese and American settings. *Chinese Journal of Communication, 1*(2), 168–180.

Herman, B. (1997, December 14). Hearing impaired present special problems, opportunities for police. *Miami Herald*, at 5B.

Hoopes, R. (2006a). Trampling Miranda: Interrogating deaf suspects. In C. Lucas (Ed.), *Language and the law in deaf communities* (p. 28). Gallaudet University Press.

Hoopes, R. (2006b). Trampling Miranda: Interrogating deaf suspects. In C. Lucas (Ed.), *Language and the law in deaf communities* (p. 22). Gallaudet University Press.

Hsu, S. (2017, October 1). D.C. jail held man for 77 days after his case was dropped until another inmate flagged an attorney. *The Washington Post*.

Lewis, T. (2014). Police brutality and deaf people. Speak Freely. American Civil Liberties Union (ACLU). Retrieved 2022, from https://www.aclu.org/blog/national-security/police-brutality-and-deaf-people

Lewis v. Truitt, 960 F. Supp. 175,176 (S.D. Ind. 1997).

Maryland v. Barker, Crim. No's. 17,995 and 19,518 (Md. Cir. Ct. Dec. 8, 1977).

McAnnany, K., & Kothekar, S. (2011). With their own hands: A community lawyering approach to improving law enforcement practices in the deaf community, 45 VAL. U. L. REV. 875.

McEntee, M. (1995). Deaf and hard-of-hearing clients: Some legal complications. *Social Work, 40*(2), 183–187.

Miranda v. Arizona, 384 U.S. 436 (1966).

Nelson, P. (2012). Awareness is key for cops, awareness. *Times-Union*. Accessed at http://www.timesunion.com/local/article/Awareness-key-for-cops-disabled3415737.ph

OIKLA. STAT. tit. 63, § 2410(A) (Supp. 2 2007).

Sandlin, S. (1995). APD, jail change handling of deaf, ALBUQUERQUE J. (N.M.), Sept. 2.

Scharper, J. (2009, March 9). Eroding a wall between police, the deaf. Tribunedigital-baltimoresun. *The Baltimore Sun*.

Sheprow, G. J. (1999, December 10). Interpreting the Miranda warnings. *American Sign Language Resources*.

Silvasi, P. M. (2020). *Warnings that fell on deaf ears: A three-pronged analysis of encounters between deaf individuals and law enforcement*. Gallaudet University.

Smith, J. (2010, December 3). Tone deaf. Deaf austinites say police can't seem to listen to reason. *The Austin Chronicle*. http://www.austinchronicle.com/news/2010-12-03/tonedeaf/

State of Oregon v. Mason, Crim. No. C 80-03-30821 (Or. Cir. Ct. May 27, 1980).

State of Tennessee v. Chester Lee Jenkins. No. E2001-01173-CCA-R9-CD (2002).

TENN. CODE ANN. § 24-1-211(3) (Supp. 2010).

Twersky-Glasner, A. (2006). Miranda warnings and deaf suspects: It is not just a matter of translation. *Criminal Law Bulletin, 42*, 593.

United States Department of Justice (USDOJ). (2019). *Miranda and the deaf suspect*. Police Executive Research Forum, Washington Bureau. Retrieved from https://www.worldcat.org/title/miranda-and-the-deaf-suspect

United States Department of Justice (USDOJ). (2020). *Communication with people who are deaf or hard of hearing: ADA guide for law enforcement officers*. Retrieved from https://search.justice.gov/search/docs?affiliate=justice&dc=3851&query=Deaf

Vernon, M., Raifman, L., & Greenberg, S. (1996a). The Miranda warnings and the deaf suspect. *Behavioral Sciences and the Law, 14*, 128.

Vernon, M., Raifman, L., & Greenberg, S. (1996b). The Miranda warnings and the deaf suspect. *Behavioral Sciences and the Law, 14*, 123.

Vernon, M., Raifman, L., & Greenberg, S. (1996c). The Miranda warnings and the deaf suspect. *Behavioral Sciences and the Law, 14*, 122.

Vernon, M., Raifman, L., Greenberg, S., & Monteiro, B. (2001). Forensic pretrial police interviews of deaf suspects avoiding legal pitfalls. *Journal of Law and Psychiatry, 24*(2021), 43–59.

Wakeland, E., Rose, J., & Austin, S. (2019). Professionals experience of deaf offenders with mental health difficulties. *American Annals of the Deaf, 164*(1), 137–157.

Wisconsin v. Hindsley. 237 Wis.2d 358. (2000). Retrieved from https://www.wicourts.gov/html/ca/99/99-1374.htm

Chapter 3
Deaf Defendants and the Legal System

3.1 Deaf Defendants in Legal Settings

As Deaf defendants make up only a small percentage of civil or criminal cases, judges, attorneys, and other courtroom personnel rarely encounter situations which require accommodations for their unique needs. They often lack familiarity with the challenges Deaf defendants experience when involved with the legal system or with the specific laws and accommodations that have been created to assure an equal and fair process (Dubow & National Association of the Deaf, 2000). While there is currently protective legislation (e.g., ADA) designed to ensure that the needs and rights of people with disabilities, as intended by the Bill of Rights, are not overlooked (Dubow & National Association of the Deaf, 2000), they are not always observed or enforced (Andrews et al., 2007; Frumkin, 1998; Musumeci, 2006; Terhune, 2004–2005). Furthermore, the legal system's lack of awareness of the needs of Deaf defendants "are frequently not recognized, albeit unintentionally" (Vernon & Andrews, 2011, p. 8). Many examples exist of the negative consequences for the Deaf defendant when courts do not enforce these laws or do not provide adequate accommodations (Thomas & Gastin, 2009; Vernon, 2010).

D. M. Feldman et al., *Intersections of the Legal System and the Deaf Community*, SpringerBriefs in Psychology, https://doi.org/10.1007/978-3-031-28100-6_3

3.2 Deaf Defendants and Attorneys

As noted above, few attorneys have any knowledge, awareness, or experience with deaf defendants. Under the ADA, attorneys cannot refuse to serve someone solely due to a disability, and attorneys are generally required to provide accommodations for a client who is deaf when asked for (42 U.S.C § 12101 et seq; 42 USC § 12181(7), 42 U.S.C. § 12181; 28 C.F.R. § 36.303(c), 28 C.F.R. § 36.303(c), 28 C.F.R. § 36.301(c). While the provision of interpreters is important, it does not increase the attorney's awareness of culture and language and the challenges these may pose related to the attorney's ability to adequately represent and advocate on behalf of the deaf client. It is highly recommended that an attorney choose to represent a Deaf client who is unfamiliar with these issues consult with other legal, mental health, and other professionals and experts who have such experience with the Deaf community as early as possible. This will help ensure that the legal rights and protections afforded the Deaf client are observed from the start and that any accommodation concerns that may affect the outcome of litigation are addressed.

Vernon and Andrews (2011, pp. 3–4) created several suggestions for attorneys working with Deaf defendants including:

1. Obtaining valid data on educational and linguistic levels, especially reading levels
2. Obtaining client IQ
3. Obtaining data on how the Miranda warnings were administered
4. Requesting interpreting be done consecutively, as opposed to simultaneously
5. Making sure deaf defendants with low language skills that a Certified Deaf Interpreter is present
6. Making sure an interpreter is available during trial for the defense attorney (if the deaf defendant signs)
7. Requesting the trial be videotaped as well as transcribed
8. Videotaping any interrogations of deaf defendants
9. Allowing CART for deaf defendants who prefer captioning rather than a sign language interpreter
10. Examining all videotapes of arrest and interrogations, which should have been recorded by the police, with the assistance of an interpreter

3.3 The Psychological Evaluation of Deaf Defendants

In litigation, psychological evaluations are often used to help determine competency and criminal responsibility. While the exact process may vary, numerous psychological factors may be measured as part of a test battery and used to analyze and eventually opine on a legal or diagnostic question. Often involved is the providing of data used to evidence the defendants' understanding of such things as "right and wrong" and their ability to conform their behaviors to the law. When performing any psychological testing, it is important to consider how cultural and linguistic factors may influence the test selection, data collection, or conclusion processes. For this reason, the psychological evaluation of Deaf defendants for legal purposes present unique challenges to both attorneys and mental health professionals (Pollard Jr. & Berlinski, 2017). Many factors need to be considered prior to beginning any forensic evaluations and may include the defendants' fund of legal knowledge; language considerations for differences, preferences, or deprivation; cultural and community connection and context; and level and type of education (O'rourke & Grewer, 2005). The forensic examiner must also consider their own competency and level of awareness of the Deaf culture, community, and language when making decisions regarding their ability to perform such evaluations. A psychologist who is aware of, and experienced with cultural and language challenges, who is knowledgeable of the various assessment resources available, and the appropriate utilization of such tools, should be at the core of any psychological evaluation. However, few psychologists who are skilled in the psychological evaluation of Deaf defendants exist, and a few evaluative resources have been developed that specifically provide for the needs of Deaf examinees (Morere et al., 2019).

An essential and crucial first step is determining the optimal communication method(s) necessary for an accurate, meaningful, and successful evaluation (Black & Glickman, 2006; Diaz et al., 2013). Legal requirements, available resources, and the preferences of the Deaf defendant with regard to communication and language should also be considered when initially making plans and arrangements for an examination. The best communication method for a psychological evaluation with a Deaf defendant, who utilizes ASL, is a psychologist trained in clinical and forensic assessment, with knowledge of Deaf culture and proficiency in ASL. However, few professionals with all three of these skills are readily available, and those that do are spread out in various locations across the United States. It is highly recommended that psychologists who do not have the combination of the skills listed above should, before taking on a psychological evaluation of a

Deaf defendant, review their own competencies and assess any challenges that may arise.

As noted previously, not all deaf individuals utilize ASL with any proficiency or at all. In these cases, a thorough analysis of language ability and communication preferences should be completed with the assistance of a professional familiar with signed language and communication systems. In addition to ASL interpreters, CDIs may need to be retained to further facilitate communication with low- or nonlanguage deaf defendants. For those deaf individuals who do not prefer signed communication and who prefer an oral or speech reading method, CART or other live captioning systems, or a combination of signed and non-signed methods, their preferences should be respected, and the examiner should accommodate the client as needed. As in all cases, these accommodations should include consultation with experts or referral to professionals with the skills to provide such accommodations. Appropriate accommodations should be made prior to initiating any evaluation, and consistency across multiple settings is essential.

In addition to the general lack of sociocultural knowledge among many hearing professionals, there is a huge gap in available evaluation materials and techniques specifically developed for use with Deaf examinees (Landsberger et al., 2013). Tests with normative data or standardized administration rules specific to Deaf defendants are extremely rare, which may leave the forensic psychologist administering, scoring, or interpreting the evaluation of a Deaf examinee based on inappropriate "hearing" norms. For many tests that do have some *deaf* norms, it is often difficult to ascertain if the sample group is Deaf or deaf, or signing or oral. Few tests have any ASL to English interpretation standards or administrative guidelines, and this is a major concern considering the need for accuracy in English to ASL translations. Even test instructions may present a challenge as some terms and concepts may not readily be translatable to accurately reflect the task or objective.

Intelligence and achievement tests that use English-based vocabulary as stimuli may not readily be translated into ASL, or other forms of signed communication, with the same intent or meaning, or the sign gives away the answer. Simply fingerspelling vocabulary words is not an appropriate solution as it may change the nature and difficulty of the test as a spelled word is not the equivalent of a signed word. Many personality tests are based on self-report following the reading of a statement, and consideration for the English reading level of the deaf examinee, often lower than hearing peers and not necessarily reflective of education level, must be considered.

Written statements above the Deaf defendants' English reading proficiency level or presented in a different word order/grammatical format than in ASL may be confusing for the Deaf examinee. Personality and adaptive functioning tests utilize scoring algorithms imbedded within the test structure which may not take into account hearing loss, sign language, or Deaf culture in how, questions, are asked or endorsements rated or scored. Therefore, it is important for the forensic psychologist to consider how hearing loss, language, or other cultural phenomena may skew the questions (e.g., "*hearing* things," "*talking to strangers,*" "*people don't understand me*") and therefore the scoring and interpretation.

Forensic psychologists evaluating Deaf suspects rely on the ASL interpreter to find the sign(s) that best communicates the concept of the English-based test question or task to the Deaf defendant—and to relay the response of the Deaf defendant from ASL to English. However, interpreters are not psychometricians and are not trained in psychological measurement or concepts. Therefore, they may *unintentionally* miss some of the nuances and subtleties of testing, alter questions based on their understanding of the task, overexplain questions, and "coach," or use, signs that give away an answer. In addition, again *unintentionally*, when translating ASL responses to English, the interpreter may add to or alter responses providing a more cohesive or clarified answer than was provided by the Deaf defendant. For optimal results, interpreters and clinicians should discuss the evaluation and communication process before testing to familiarize the clinician with the role of the interpreter and to familiarize the interpreter with the nature and process of the evaluation (Landsberger et al., 2013).

Cultural differences will also play an important role in the psychological evaluations of Deaf defendants, and the significance of culture may be lost on the unaware psychologist. Such factors as personal disclosures (of both the examiner and examinee), eye contact, physical space and movement, and direct vs. indirect (e.g., through an interpreter) communication may affect both the Deaf defendant's willingness to cooperate during an evaluation and the examiner's ability to collect accurate information. Cultural awareness is critical to accurate and meaningful interpretations and the recognition of personality characteristics and attributes as psychopathology vs. "normal for deaf." Deaf defendants evaluated by forensic psychologists with no or little understanding Deaf cultural factors may be at great risk of being misdiagnosed. "Hearing bias" may incorrectly pathologize deafness through assumptions (e.g., *"how could a person who is deaf not be depressed?"*). Observed, background, or informant data taken without cultural or linguistic context might suggest isolative or asocial behavior as opposed to a lack of availability or opportunity for social interaction with other deaf or signing peers. Frustrations with communication with the examiner may be interpreted as anger or self-control problems. Culturally appropriate "gestures," such as head nodding, may be interpreted as consent, admission, or agreement. The expressive and gestural nature of sign language may be off-putting to the examiner unfamiliar with Deaf culture and sign language and therefore lead to the assumption of psychopathology. Some areas where this has been noted are as follows:

- Deaf examinees may score artificially high on measures of paranoia or paranoid symptomology. However, it is important to note that this may be due to oppression and real experiences and interactions with hearing society (Williams & Abeles, 2004). Question such as, or related to, "I often feel like people are watching me" or "No one understands me" may be reflective of actual experiences in a hearing world as opposed to genuine suspiciousness. In addition, much of observed suspiciousness may be the result of experiences "of maltreatment due to cultural/ethnic distrust, a reflection of the deaf person to monitor the environment visually" (Morere et al., 2019, p. 9).
- Glickman (2008) notes that Deaf individuals who have not developed language proficiency may appear to demonstrate symptoms of what appear to be a mistaken form of behavioral and language symptoms of psychosis. While it is possible for Deaf individuals, even those deaf from birth, to experience psychosis, including auditory hallucinations (Briffa, 1999), there are a number of other factors that should be investigated and reviewed. For example, some deaf individuals with residual hearing may misinterpret "sounds" as illusions (Tanriverdi et al., 2001). Deaf defendants may also experience visual hallucinations involving "seeing signing," such as Jesus or an image signing to them (Haskins, 2000). Glickman (2007) cautions against using hearing clinical terminology and norms to interpret the client's experience as communication and communication skills may lead to a misdiagnosis of psychosis. Additionally, psychologists should note the importance of distinguishing psychotic symptoms from those of a language dysfluency (Glickman, 2008). Some symptoms, such as lack of referents, tangentiality, circumstantiality, and neologisms, have been observed in nonpsychotic Deaf populations (Trumbetta et al., 2001). In some cases, culturally Deaf appropriate behaviors such as projecting emotions into signing and facial expressions (beyond what is expected for hearing peers) such as tapping furniture or people to get attention, vocal noises, or eye contact may be seen as bizarre or psychotic. Additionally, what may be equally as common are deaf individuals who are psychotic but whose illness is overlooked by clinicians who attribute symptoms to poor interpretation, deafness, or minimal language skills (Pollard, 2005).

- What may appear to be cognitive limitations may be due to deficits in language development, poor education, or language acquisition (Woolfe et al., 2002) and not necessarily an underlying cognitive deficit or pathological condition. A lack of information or knowledge of important personal or family-related historical information, due to poor communication with hearing parents or other family members, may be interpreted as memory or cognitive impairment.
- The inexperienced and unaware psychologist who does not understand or follow the rules of Deaf culture may alienate or frustrate the Deaf examinee. This in turn may cause the Deaf examinee to become suspicious, guarded, or less motivated to participate in the evaluation. Even if communication is fully accessible through a qualified interpreter, the diagnostic process can be compromised if the forensic psychologist is not familiar with issues commonly experienced by Deaf adults (Black & Glickman, 2006; Diaz et al., 2013).

Tests that are inappropriate, or inappropriately used, with Deaf defendants will likely yield faulty interpretations. As in other situations, forensic psychologists evaluating Deaf defendants are required by ethical standards to be aware of the reliability and validity of the tests they choose and the competent interpretation of the results. Even for those psychologists trained and experienced in the evaluation of Deaf defendants, test selection, administration, and interpretation of testing materials will likely depend heavily on individual knowledge, experience, and clinical judgment. Forensic psychologists evaluating Deaf defendants may have to break with administration and protocol to accommodate the Deaf examinee (Maller, 2003), and it is important to take into account how any adaptations may have affected results. Any modifications or adaptations to test materials must be done with extreme caution and only by psychologists trained and experienced with the examination of Deaf defendants. Any modifications or accommodations must be noted in the report with the rationale and potential ramifications to interpretation provided.

3.4 Deaf Defendants and Legal Knowledge

Deaf defendants are afforded the same legal and due process protections under the constitution as their hearing counterparts. However, they may not have equal access to those protections due to disparities in communication, cultural awareness, and the lack of knowledgeable professionals with experience in recognizing the special needs, circumstances, and accommodations of the deaf defendant (Vernon & Raifman, 1997). One central legal concept that is often difficult to ascertain with Deaf defendants is the evaluation of competency to proceed (Davidson, et al., 2015). Dusky v. United States (1960) states that a (competent) defendant "has sufficient mental ability to consult with his attorney with a reasonable degree of rational understanding and with a factual understanding of the charges and proceedings against him." Considering the underlying challenges of language and communication experienced by many deaf defendants, they are at a likely disadvantage when competency is evaluated. To further complicate matters, many deaf individuals, because of linguistic disadvantages, have experienced less access to education and a lower fund of knowledge, especially regarding legal terminology and concepts. Miller and Vernon (2001) looked specifically at linguistic diversity and the legal system and noted that "between 25 and 40 percent of prelingually deaf or hard of hearing persons are at risk for being found incompetent to stand trial" due to what King and Vernon (1999) defined an "insufficient primitive linguistic level" (page 99). Additionally, Miller (2004) found that 50% of deaf inmates in a Texas prison had limited reading and language abilities severe enough to question their understanding of due process during their arrest and trial. Miller, Vernon, and Capella (2005) also found that 20.2% of violent deaf offenders in a prison population possessed minimal language skills severe enough to argue that they should have been deemed incompetent to stand trial.

Individual knowledge and ability will vary with each individual and be based on such factors as education, language development, socialization, connection to the Deaf community, and onset of hearing loss. However, similar to their hearing counterparts, it is often those deaf individuals with the lowest education, language ability, and social connectiveness who are the ones most likely to come into contact with the legal system (Lochner, 2020). They are also the most likely to have negative legal outcomes because of their inability to comprehend complex legal information and to use that information to make informed decisions (Miller, 2004). The Deaf defendant may have such a meager knowledge of English, as well as ASL, that it becomes extremely difficult to convey to them their due process rights (Holmes v Florida, 1985; Vernon & Miller, 2001). Deaf defendants may have a difficult time with words and concepts that have no signed equivalent or with terms that are unfamiliar in common discourse (e.g., "charges" or "range of possible penalties"). Other examples include legal terms, such as there being no ASL sign for *competency* that expresses the definition of the term in a purely legal or forensic context. In fact, the closest sign that would likely be used in a rough translation would be *skilled*, but that is not how the word is meant in this context. Incomplete or inadequate translations will likely affect how the deaf suspect or defendant will conceptualize their situation and therefore limit their understanding, ability to provide informed consent, or the options available to them. The plea of *no contest* could be interpreted by unqualified or inexperienced interpreters as *no/not competition* which may indicate or suggest the sense of a "game" or an option "not to participate" to the Deaf defendant. The concepts of "guilt" and "innocence" may be misunderstood or misinterpreted as "bad" and "good" which cause confusion regarding the Deaf defendants understanding of pleas and ability to communicate with their attorney or the court. Other legal terms have no signed equivalent (e.g., jury), and when a substitution is utilized (e.g., using fingerspelling, or "decision group"), it may not convey the same meaning. This can be made more confusing as different sign language interpreters may use different signs, or signing styles, for the same term or concept. In these, as well as in other examples, the legal and contextual meaning of the term is lost and therefore limits the ability of the Deaf defendant to understand the legal process and make an informed decision.

Similar to other forensic examinations, the evaluation of competency for deaf defendants can be a complex and challenging process. Even psychologists trained and experienced in doing forensic evaluations find there is little in the way of resources specific to this population. Competency evaluations utilizing more standardized methods based on English or non-deaf norms may not be an efficient means to evaluate competency in Deaf defendants. It would not be appropriate to use tests with Deaf individuals with a reading level below what is required by test administration rules. Some tests may have concepts which are difficult to translate from English to ASL and, even when translated by qualified interpreter, may not convey comparable meaning. As noted above almost no evaluative materials exist that are normed on Deaf populations or designed to be used specifically with Deaf defendants. Competency assessment tools typically range from semi-structured interviews (CCAP, FIT) to more highly structured and standardized questions pertaining to specific aspects of legal knowledge (ECST-R, MacCAT-CA). In both cases, the ability of the Deaf defendant to accurately comprehend the questions may be impacted by language, interpreting, and cultural differences. In cases where more unstructured, or semi-structured, interviews are used to assess competency, much relies on the ability of the examiner to formulate questions which are meaningful and interpretable and therefore understood by the defendant. When interpreters must be relied on, which changes communication to a less efficient indirect method, the psychologist's ability to assess the Deaf defendant's competency may be compromised by ASL interpreters' *unintentional* misunderstandings of the purpose of the competency evaluation or the lack of familiarity with legal terms and concepts.

Considering these limitations, it becomes extremely difficult to establish if the deaf defendant has a minimum fund of knowledge as required by law to demonstrate competency and, if not, to determine if competency is a restorable condition. For those deemed not competent, but restorable, consideration must be made for an appropriate restoration environment. This should include a professional with sign language ability and knowledge of Deafness or, if no such person is available, the use of interpreters or other accommodations as *preferred by the deaf individual.* Individual training may also be more effective as competency groups typically will focus on spoken English with facilitators and participants that do not sign or accommodate the Deaf participant. Furthermore, restoration training should demonstrate actual knowledge as the rote memorization of English-based legal terms would not likely be enough to demonstrate competency for a deaf defendant under US v. Duhon (2000).

3.5 American Sign Language Interpreters in Legal Settings

Care and consideration for the needs and preferences of the Deaf defendant must be factored in the determining the effectiveness of an ASL interpreter. It is often assumed that in cases of the Deaf defendants, simply providing an ASL interpreter will provide equal access to court proceedings; however, "for a number of reasons, nothing could be farther from the truth" (Vernon & Andrews, 2011, p. 6). While there are certainly some Deaf defendants who would have no difficulty demonstrating competency and following the court proceedings with the aid of an ASL interpreter, many Deaf defendants have such limited language ability that any form of communication accommodation would be inadequate. Vernon and Miller (2001) suggest that "such cases represent linguistic incompetence to stand trial, just as mental retardation and legal insanity represent psychological incompetence" and references Holmes v Florida (1986) as a case example. It is also important for clinicians to be mindful that when a Deaf defendant exhibits low language ability, a CDI should retained to further break down concepts and facilitate communication.

The recognition of the need for accommodations for Deaf defendants has been implied by early legal decisions as part of "due process" and "fair opportunity to defend oneself against the state's accusations" rights (Chambers v. Mississippi, 1973). Vasquez v. State (1991) included the right to "trial proceedings interpreted into a language that a defendant can understand." In addition, there are requirements that a defendant be more than "physically present," "be informed about the proceedings so he or she can assist in the defense," and that they be provided "a meaningful opportunity to present a complete defense" (State v. Caldron, 2000; Hawkins v. Costello, 2006). While none of these are specific to Deaf defendants, the implication is that more than just basic and simple communication is required and access to a qualified interpreter is necessary to ensure a complete defense. More specifically for the Deaf defendant, the Sixth Amendment right to participate in one's own defense has been interpreted to include the right to "accommodations for impairments" and that there exists "the right to have a competent translator assist him…throughout his trial" (United States ex Rel. Negron v. State of N.Y., 1970).

Several pieces of US legislation have focused on providing accommodations for people during legal proceedings. In 1978, the United States Congress passed the Court Interpreters Act (28 U.S.C.A. § 1827) to provide for more effective use of interpreters in federal court, as well as to address the certification and appointment of interpreters in federal judicial proceedings as to address the certification and appointment of interpreters in federal judicial proceedings (40 A.L.R. Fed. 2d 115, 2009). The Court Interpreter Act ensures that defendants who are not sufficiently competent in the English language understand the judicial proceedings against them. While the Court Interpreters Act initially only protect the rights of defendants in federal criminal cases, court interpreting occurs also at the district court level (FCIM, 2014). In order to protect the rights of defendants in state courts, the Supreme Court affirmed that "Title VI prohibition against national origin discrimination includes discrimination against individuals on the basis of language" (Language Access in State Courts, 2016).

In 1978, the Bilingual, Hearing, and Speech-Impaired Court Interpreter Act was adopted by federal court for any civil or criminal action. This required that a qualified interpreter be provided by the court in which a deaf, speech-impaired, or non-English-speaking person must participate (BHSICIA, 1978). In 1988, Public Law 100–702, the Judicial Improvements and Access to Justice Act made several amendments to the Court Interpreters Act, including the use of interpreters in grand jury and pretrial proceedings. As previously noted above, a further piece of legislation, the Americans with Disabilities Act (ADA, 1990), also addresses reasonable accommodation which must be provided to people with disabilities in various settings. These requirements were further expanded through Executive Order 13166: Improving Access to Services for Persons with Limited English Proficiency (LEP) in August 2000.

3.6 Conclusion

In some cases, utilizing a ASL interpreter may provide necessary access for more language-proficient and better-educated Deaf defendants. However, other factors such as language or cognitive deficits may be more difficult to accommodate and may require the services of a CDI and consultation with experts. In some cases, the expressive nature of sign language and the vocalizations made by some deaf individuals (who cannot hear these vocalizations) may suggest the inability to conform their behavior to a courtroom setting or to maintain appropriate courtroom behavior. It is important to recognize what behaviors for a deaf defendant are typical and appropriate with regard to both "normal for deaf" and Deaf culture. These should be distinguished from truly uncontrollable, pathological, or intentionally disruptive behaviors that are atypical for deaf individuals and Deaf culture. While certainly knowledge of sign language and communication is important for the evaluation of competency, equal awareness of cultural factors and their impact must also be considered.

References

Administrative Office of the United States Courts, Court Services Office. (2014). *Federal court interpreter orientation manual and glossary*. https://www.uscourts.gov/sites/default/files/federal-court-interpreter-orientation-manual_0.pdf

Americans with Disabilities Act of 1990, PUb. L. No. 101–336, 104 Stat. 328 (1990) § 35.160.

Andrews, J. F., Vernon, M., & LaVigne, M. (2007). The Bill of Rights, due process and the deaf suspect. *Journal of Interpreting, 2007*, 9–38.

BHSICIA (1978). H.R. 12003 — 95th Congress: Bilingual, Hearing and Speech Impaired Court Interpreter Act. www.GovTrack.us. April 1, 2023.

Black, P. A., & Glickman, N. S. (2006). Demographics, psychiatric diagnoses, and other characteristics of North American deaf and hard-of-hearing inpatients. *Journal of Deaf Studies and Deaf Education, 11*, 303–321. https://doi.org/10.1093/deafed/enj042

Briffa, D. (1999). *Hallucinations in deaf people with mental illness: Lessons from the deaf client*. Retrieved September 9, 2006, www.qds.org.au/mentalhealth

Davidson, F., Kovacevic, V., Cave, M., Hart, K., & Dark, F. (2015). Assessing fitness for trial of deaf defendants. *Psychiatry, Psychology and Law, 22*(1), 145–156. https://doi.org/10.1080/13218719.2014.919690

Diaz, D. R., Landsberger, S. A., Povlinski, J., Sheward, J., & Sculley, C. (2013). Psychiatric disorder prevalence among deaf and hard-of-hearing outpatients. *Comprehensive Psychiatry, 54*, 991–995. https://doi.org/10.1016/j.comppsych.2013.04.004

DuBow, S., & National Association of the Deaf. (2000). *Legal rights: The guide for deaf and hard of hearing people* (5th ed.). Gallaudet University Press.

Frumkin, I. B. (1998). *Competency to waive Miranda Rights* (pp. 8–9). NLADA Indigent Defense.

Glickman, N. (2007). Do you hear voices? Problems in assessment of mental status in deaf persons with severe language deprivation. *Journal of Deaf Studies and Deaf Education, 12*, 127–147.

Glickman, N. (2008). *Cognitive-behavioral therapy for deaf and hearing persons with language and learning challenges*. Routledge.

Haskins, B. M. D. (2000, December). Serving and assessing deaf patients: Implications for psychiatry. *Psychiatric Times* (Vol. XVII, Issue 12).

Holmes, Steven, Appelant v the State of Florida, Appellee #83-1055, District Court of Appeals of Florida, Third District (August 12, 1986).

King, N., & Vernon, M. (1999). Unique legal issues facing deaf defendants. *The Florida Defender, VII*(#1), 11–15.

Landsberger, S. A., Sajid, A., Schmelkin, L., Diaz, D. R., & Weiler, C. (2013). Assessment and treatment of deaf adults with psychiatric disorders: A review of the literature for practitioners. *Journal of Psychiatric Practice, 19*(2), 87–97.

Lochner, L. (2020). Education of crime. In S. Bradley & C. Green (Eds.), *The economics of education* (2nd ed.). Academic.

Maller, S. J. (2003). Intellectual assessment of deaf people: A critical review of core concepts and issues. In M. Marshark & P. E. Spencer (Eds.), *Oxford handbook of deaf studies, language, and education* (pp. 451–463). Oxford University Press.

Miller, K. (2004). Linguistic diversity in a Deaf prison population: implications for due process. *Journal of Deaf Studies and Deaf Education, 9*(1), 112–119.

Miller, K. R., & Vernon, M. (2001). Linguistic diversity in deaf defendants and due process. *Journal of Deaf Studies and Deaf Education, 6*(#3), 226–234.

Miller, K. R., Vernon, M., & Capella, M. E. (2005). Violent offenders in a deaf prison population. *Journal of Deaf Studies and Deaf Education, 10*(4), 417–425.

Morere, D. A., Dean, P. M., & Mompremoer, L. (2019). Mental health assessment of deaf clients: Issues with interpreters use and assessment of person with diminished capacity and psychiatric populations. *JADARA, 42*(4), 9.

Musumeci, M. B. (2006). Confronting sentences that silence: The Americans with Disabilities Act: Effective communication mandate for prisoners and probationers who are deaf. *Clearinghouse Review Journal of Poverty, Law and Policy, 2006*, 627–638.

O'rourke, S., & Grewer, G. (2005). Assessment of deaf people in forensic mental health settings: A risky business! *The Journal of Forensic Psychiatry & Psychology, 16*(4), 671–684. https://doi.org/10.1080/14789940500279877

Pollard, R. (2005). *Psychological testing studies: Psychosis symptom rating scale*. Deaf Health Task Force. University of Rochester School of Medicine.

Pollard, R. Q., Jr., & Berlinski, B. T. (2017). Forensic Evaluation of Deaf Individuals: Challenges and Strategies. *Journal of Social Work in Disability & Rehabilitation, 16*(3-4), 261–275. https://doi.org/10.1080/1536710X.2017.1372240

Tanriverdi, N., Sayilgan, M. A., & Özçürümez, G. (2001). Musical hallucinations associated with abmptly developed bilateral loss of hearing. *Acta Psychiatrica Scandinavica, 103*(2), 153–155.

Terhune, K. L. (2004–2005). Deaf criminal defendants: Is the system just? *National Association of the Deaf Magazine, 4*(5), 20–21.

Thomas, V. L., & Gastin, L. A. (2009). The Americans with Disabilities Act: Shattered aspirations and new hope. *Journal of the American Medical Association, 301*(1), 95.

Trumbetta, S. L., Bonvillian, J. D., Siedlecki, T., & Haskins, B. G. (2001). Language-related symptoms in persons with schizophrenia and how deaf persons may manifest these symptoms. *Sign Language Studies, 1*(3), 228–253.

U.S. Department of Justice Civil Rights Division, Federal Coordination and Compliance Section. (2016). *Language access in state courts.* https://www.justice.gov/crt/file/892036/download

US v. Duhon. (2000).

Vernon, M. (2010). The horror of being deaf and in prison. *American Annals of the Deaf, 155*(3).

Vernon, M., & Andrews, J. (2011). *Basic legal issues in handling cases of defendants who are deaf.* The Champion. National Association of Criminal Defense Lawyers.

Vernon, M., & Miller, K. (2001). Linguistic incompetence to stand trial: A unique condition in some deaf defendants. *Journal of Interpreting, Millennial Edition*, 99–120.

Vernon, M., & Raifman, L. (1997). Recognizing and handling problems of incompetent deaf defendants charged with serious crimes. *International Journal of Law and Psychiatry, 20*(3), 373–387.

Williams, C., & Abeles, N. (2004). Issues and implications of deaf culture in therapy. *Professional Psychology: Research & Practice, 35*(6), 643–648.

Woolfe, T., Want, S. C., & Siegal, M. (2002). Siblings and theory of mind in deaf native signing children. *Journal of Deaf Studies and Deaf Education, 5*(3), 342–347.

Chapter 4
Deaf Inmates and Correctional Settings

4.1 Deaf Inmates in Prison

According to the US Bureau of Justice Statistics, as of 2016, an estimated 38% of state and federal inmates have a disability and were about two and a half times more likely to report a disability than adults in the US general population (15%) (Maruschak et al., 2021). Although the experiences of many minority groups in the correctional system have been examined, little attention or study has been completed related to the experiences of Deaf inmates (Kelly, 2017). It has been estimated that tens of thousands of Deaf inmates are in the correctional system (Lewis, 2014). However, with the broad definition of deaf, hearing tests not being a typical part of the intake process, and inmate fears of being identified as deaf, correctional systems may have no accurate count of how many inmates are deaf or where they are located within the system (Gibbs & Ackerman, 1999). As being Deaf is not visually apparent, the correctional facility to which the inmate is assigned does not know the inmate is Deaf when assigning a cell, cellmate(s), work details, recreational time, or other facility activities.

While the literature specific to Deaf inmates is incomplete, it has been well documented that for other settings, specialized training and knowledge are essential in order to work successfully with Deaf people at various stages of the judicial process. Prison can be an extremely difficult process for the Deaf inmate as correctional facilities are not designed or equipped for their needs (Gibbs & Ackerman, 1999). Deaf individuals held within the correctional system present a unique challenge for administration, staff, correctional officers, and other professionals. In general, accommodations should

D. M. Feldman et al., *Intersections of the Legal System and the Deaf Community*, SpringerBriefs in Psychology, https://doi.org/10.1007/978-3-031-28100-6_4

be provided for any critical communication, complex information distribution, lengthy exchanges, or anything involving legal or other due processes. In addition, daily activities, treatment, rehabilitation, and other facets of correctional life will likely be impacted by the Deaf inmate's special needs.

As noted previously, Deaf inmates with the least amount of education and language ability are also those most likely to be incarcerated with one study showing that 50% of deaf inmates in a Texas prison had limited reading and language abilities (Miller, 2004). In another study, also in a Texas prison, all 99 Deaf inmates had an average educational level of 2 years and 4 months, were functionally illiterate, and had intelligible speech (Miller, 2001; Miller & Vernon, 2001). In some situations, Deaf inmates may be unaware of their situation or conditions of their incarceration (Ridgeway, 2012). As so many Deaf inmates likely have impoverished reading levels and are unable to communicate effectively (Miller & Vernon, 2001), they may not be able to understand written facility rules, information, and expectations. Interpreters are rarely provided at orientations, and distributed handbooks are typically far beyond the reading level of all but a few Deaf inmates (Goben et al., 2009). Without access to such important information, Deaf inmates are likely to have difficulty navigating the complexities of a correctional institution, and this may put Deaf inmates in conflict with correctional staff and fellow inmates (Miller, 2001; Miller & Vernon, 2001). Such information may be critical to following rules and procedures and even survival while in prison. As inmates may face disciplinary consequences if they do not respond to orally presented orders or sound-based cues, Deaf inmates may find themselves constantly facing disciplinary actions (Miller, 2001; Miller & Vernon, 2001). Assumptions may be made that the Deaf inmate is able to lip-read or speak, and when they are not able to communicate in this way, it may be interpreted as defiance. In addition, Deaf inmates are highly vulnerable to assault by other inmates who see them as isolated, unable to report offenses, or unaware of their surroundings (Feldman, 2017).

4.2 Deaf Inmates and Accommodations

The lack of accommodations while incarcerated poses a significant problem for Deaf inmates and is often attributed to a lack of awareness or limited resources on the part of correctional staff (Feldman, 2017). The types of accommodations correctional facilities may be required to provide to ensure Deaf inmates can communicate and function effectively are not limited to interpreters which are typically provided only for specific activities. Services and provisions may need to include visual alert systems that inform inmates of announcements or emergencies made by loudspeaker, visual or vibrating alarms, hearing aids and batteries for hearing aids, and CART or other captioning systems as preferred by the deaf inmate. Further, Deaf inmates may be entitled by law to these types of accommodations in a wide variety of correctional activities including religious services, medical consultations, and disciplinary hearings (Musumerci, 2006). The choice of the most effective accommodation(s) must be made in consultation with the input of the Deaf inmate and should be discussed at intake into the correction facility, if not planned beforehand.

4.3 The Legal Rights of Deaf Inmates

Deaf inmates have constitutional and statutory rights to access to correctional facilities. However, Deaf people serving prison terms may be denied basic due process rights and access to rehabilitation programs and other prison services because there exists a failure to understand accommodation needs in prisons (Musumerci, 2006; Terhue, 2004–2005; Tucker, 1988), as well as mental health facilities (Geer, 2003; Vernon & Leigh, 2007).

Section 504 of the Rehabilitation Act of 1973 (29 U.S.C. § 794) guarantees persons with disabilities equal access to any entity that receives federal financial assistance, either directly or indirectly. Under this regulation, a Deaf inmate has a right to be provided with qualified interpreter services to enable him or her to participate in or benefit from programs and services the prison offers other inmates, as well as at any disciplinary or other proceedings. The United States Department of Justice defines the obligations that correctional facilities have to provide in order to accommodate deaf inmates and states:

> [D]etention and correctional agencies must ensure that their programs and activities are accessible to handicapped persons. For example, correctional agencies should provide for the availability of qualified interpreters (certified, where possible, by a recognized certification agency) to enable hearing-impaired inmates to participate on an equal basis with non-handicapped inmates in the rehabilitation programs offered by the correctional agencies (e.g., educational programs). 45 Fed. Reg. 37630 (1980)

Title II of the Americans with Disabilities Act (ADA), 42 U.S.C. § 12,141 et seq., then extended these rights to inmates in all state and local facilities. Title II (1991) clarifies the requirements of Section 504, and extends them to institutions that do not receive federal financial assistance. Title II regulations define the term “qualified interpreter” to mean “an interpreter who is able to interpret effectively, accurately and impartially both receptively and expressively, using any necessary specialized vocabulary" (28 C.F.R. § 35.104). The ADA Title II regulations also identify the auxiliary aids and services which a state or local correctional facility may have to provide:

> [q]ualified interpreters, notetakers, computer-aided transcription services, written materials, telephone handset amplifiers, assistive listening devices, assistive listening systems, telephones compatible with hearing aids, closed caption decoders, open and closed captioning, telecommunication devices for deaf persons (TDDs) [also called teletypewriters or TTYs], videotext displays, or other effective methods of making aurally delivered materials available to individuals with hearing impairments. (28 C.F.R. § 35.104)

Policies and procedures may have to be modified, in order to give deaf inmates access to accessible accommodations that are equal to what other inmates are provided. There must also be allowances for sufficient time to use the device as these conversations may take longer than spoken conversations. For example, if a facility has a rule that limits inmate telephone use to 15 min, they may need to extend this time for a deaf inmate using a TTY. The facility must also ensure that the deaf and hard-of-hearing inmates have the same hours of access to accessible telephone service as do other inmates. For example, some facilities limit TTY use to daytime hours because the office where a TTY is stored is only open during those hours. This violates the ADA if other inmates can make telephone calls during evening or weekend hours. No appointments or written requests to use the TTY should be required, if the same is not required for other inmates to use a telephone. Finally, some facilities prohibit inmates from using toll-free "800" numbers or "711" access numbers to reach a telecommunications relay service. These policies must be changed to enable deaf and hard-of-hearing inmates to reach the statewide TTY or other relay services, mandated by Title IV of the ADA. Relay services enable communication between a deaf or hard-of-hearing person and a person who uses a telephone. Deaf and hard-of-hearing inmates must have access to relay services.

Recently the US Supreme Court has held that states could be liable under Title II of the ADA for this kind of unconstitutional conduct (Musumerci, 2006). The cases involved were the United States v. Georgia and Goodman v. Georgia (126 S. Ct. 877 (2006)). In 2008, the US Department of Justice proposed new rules for Title II of the Americans with Disabilities Act (ADA), which apply to state and local governments.

Because these services were available to other prisoners and the prison failed to provide the accommodations necessary to make them available to deaf prisoners, the prison was liable. (For other cases involving deaf people and laws relevant to them, see Musumerci, 2006.) Complaints can be filed with the US Department of Justice (Civil Rights Division). Litigation However, the Prison Litigation Reform Act of 1995 places limitations on inmates seeking federal remedies for prison civil rights violations (42 U.S.C. § 1997(e)(a)). Most importantly, inmates may not pursue federal claims until they have exhausted all available administrative remedies. Therefore, before filing a lawsuit, Deaf inmates should make sure they have already attempted to resolve their complaint through the appropriate prison complaint procedures.

4.4 Deaf Inmates, Physical Danger, and Isolation

According to Vernon and Miller (2005), the two most serious problems deaf inmates face are physical danger and isolation. Because deaf inmates cannot hear what is going on around them and identify potentially dangerous situations, they are at a higher risk of rape and other forms of assault (Ezekiel, 1994). One reason for this is that they are viewed as being unable to report instances in which they are victimized due to their communications limitations as outlined below (Miller, 2001; Miller & Vernon, 2001; Vernon & Miller, 2005). It is also more difficult for the deaf inmate, due to language barriers, to make friends and form alliances with other inmates for mutual protection (Feldman, 2017). As being deaf makes an inmate more vulnerable to assault, many Deaf inmates may attempt to conceal their hearing loss from the inmate population (Vernon, 2010). Although the desire to be seen as not vulnerable is not unique to the Deaf inmate, it is recognized as being particularly important, as weakness associated with hearing loss is likely to make the inmate more susceptible to bullying (Crewe, 2009). Correctional facilities must also ensure that Deaf inmates who have hearing disabilities are restrained in a manner that permits effective communication (e.g., they can sign, or write) unless legitimate safety concerns dictate otherwise.

The Deaf inmate will likely experience higher levels of isolation from family, attorneys, and friends than hearing counterparts. Educational, vocational, religious, and mental health programs may also be inaccessible to the Deaf inmate due to communication difficulties and interpreter or other accommodation restrictions (Vernon, 2010). Except in larger and more populated correctional facilities an inmate who is Deaf is likely to be the only such in that facility (Novic, 2018). Even if they do sign, the likelihood of other signing inmates, correctional staff, or medical or mental health providers is low, and any real socialization may be nonexistent. Deaf inmates may not be provided full access to necessary accommodations on a consistent enough basis that would serve to lessen some of the isolation experienced (Vernon, 2010). Correctional facilities typically do not have sign language interpreters on staff or available on a daily basis and like many law enforcement agencies contract with interpreter agencies on an as-needed basis and must be scheduled in advance.

4.5 Deaf Inmates and Psychopathology in Correctional Settings

Isolation and a lack of socialization in correctional settings may lead to higher and more severe rates of mental disorders such as depression, anxiety, and paranoia (Jeanne, 2013). Deaf inmates may experience mental, social, and emotional consequences of imprisonment more severely than hearing inmates as a result of the correctional facilities' inability, or unwillingness, to accommodate their needs. Accessible mental health services, or social support, available to the hearing inmates may not be available to the deaf inmate if accommodations are not provided. This leaves the deaf inmate either without treatment or provided treatment with such minimal communication that is ineffective and meaningless (Miller, 2001; Miller & Vernon, 2001). When mental health programs are accessible to deaf inmates, there are few professionals who can communicate directly with the inmate or with any knowledge of the specific needs of deaf inmates, Deaf culture, and who also have experience working with correctional settings (Feldman, 2017).

An additional complication arises from misperception of the culturally appropriate behaviors of the Deaf inmates as indicative of pathology. Deaf inmates may experience high levels of frustration due to the difficulties with communication, and their behaviors (e.g., tapping or banging to get attention, large gestures to emphasize emotional content) may then be mistaken for evidence of a mental disorder, aggression, or defiance, which could then lead to disciplinary actions (Feldman, 2017). In contrast, Deaf inmates who are isolative, due to communication limitations, could be mistaken for depressed. Inability to follow rules or instructions could be perceived as limited cognitive functioning, as opposed to communication deficits which limit communication and comprehension. Interactions between deaf inmates and correctional officers may be complicated by facial expressions and body language which could be interpreted as hostile or aggressive. Other culturally based expressions, such as head nodding, may be perceived as agreement or assent, creating the belief that the deaf inmate understands, admit, or agrees with what is being said. Such challenges can become especially problematic if the deaf inmate fails to obey the verbal commands of correctional officers when these are interpreted as defiance and not a communication issue (e.g., verbally being ordered to remain still missed by the deaf inmate because they did not hear the command).

4.6 Deaf Visitors to Correctional Facilities

Visitors with disabilities often face hindrances and barriers when trying to visit an inmate because the facility fails to accommodate their disabilities. Barriers include a lack of accessible parking, inaccessible entrances and visitation areas, and lack of effective communication or a modification of policy that would make the facility accessible to the visitor. Correctional facilities cannot require that the visitor bring their own interpreter (Ballinger & Nguyen, 2019). The facility must also provide disabled visitors auxiliary aids or services, when needed, so they can participate in all visitor services and programs. Inmates or visitors who may need accommodations may include people who are deaf, deafblind, hard of hearing, blind or have low vision, and have speech-related disabilities or cognitive and intellectual disabilities.

4.7 American Sign Language Interpreters and Other Accommodations in Correctional Settings

The failure to provide, or inaccessibility of, accommodations while incarcerated is a violation of both ADA rights and a violation of personal safety (Miller, 2002). The lack of accommodations while incarcerated poses a significant problem to the Deaf inmate and can be attributed to a lack of cultural understanding or limited resources (Grossman, 2015). Interactions in which "the risks of miscommunication or misunderstanding are high, and the consequences of miscommunication may have serious consequences for inmates" are often referred to as "high stakes interactions" (McBride V. Michigan Department of Corrections, 2018) and were first applied in the Holmes v. Baldwin settlement (Holmes, et al. v. Balwin, 2018). Deaf individuals have the right to access anything the general inmate population can access, including work opportunities, recreational activities, and making phone calls. Accommodations such as light-based alarms and information presented in a way the majority of Deaf inmates can understand are frequently unavailable, either because of costs or staff not being familiar with the need, or existence, of such accommodations. The civil rights outlined in the American with Disabilities Act pertaining to inmates with disabilities are often ignored, or at least not enforced by correctional officials, law enforcement agencies, and the courts (Vernon, 2009). Available accommodations and technology are often not provided due to a lack of systematic awareness of the needs or rights of Deaf inmates in correctional settings (Kelly, 2017). As there is no unified method in place to log hearing status of individuals who encounter the justice system, there is no efficient way to track the accommodations actively being employed within the system at any given time (Miller et al., 2005).

However, the inability to access such opportunities in these settings is often the result of not having access to ASL interpreters. This lack of qualified ASL interpreters in almost all US jails and prisons leaves most inmates who are Deaf unaware of critical information needed for safety and survival in prison (Miller, 2001; Miller & Vernon, 2001; Vernon, 2009). Despite federal laws dictating the use of interpreters in correctional settings, a 1993 survey found that almost 40% of the responding agencies did not provide interpreters even though 72% indicated they served Deaf people (McEntee, 1993). This will often result in Deaf inmates being uninformed regarding rules, safety, and day-to-day information in correctional facilities (Ridgeway, 2012).

The lack of available qualified interpreters may leave the deaf inmate at a disadvantage in information critical for safety and survival (Miller, 2001; Miller & Vernon, 2001; Vernon, 2009). Without an interpreter, the Deaf inmate may not have the ability to communicate with correctional officers, administrators, and other inmates. They may not be able to fully participate in rehabilitation, educational, religious, social, and activities, including visitation with attorneys and loved ones.

Unfortunately, a commonly used "easy" solution in an effort to save money and time used in some correctional facilities is the enlisting of the aid of a (hearing) inmate who "knows" sign language to serve as an interpreter. This may include at such important functions such as disciplinary hearings, treatment meetings, medical examinations, orientations, and visitations (Vernon, 2010). It cannot be overstated that the substitution of a qualified ASL interpreter for any nonqualified person is inappropriate and can lead to negative, harmful, or even life-threatening consequences for the deaf inmate. First, inmate interpreters have no obligation to any ethical guidelines, including maintaining confidentiality, nor serious penalties for mistakes, or intentional misinterpretations. They may create a serious danger by passing private information on to other inmates or exploitation by using such information against the deaf inmate in extortion or blackmail schemes. Miller, 2001; Miller & Vernon, 2001 reported at least one documented case where an inmate interpreter put a deaf inmate in physical danger when they leaked information about the deaf inmate's crime to the general population. Second, inmate interpreters may not have the sign language skills to accurately facilitate communication. Third, inmate interpreters may intentionally distort communication between correctional staff and the deaf inmate for their own needs (Vernon, 2010).

Recommendations for improving the access to the correctional facility for Deaf inmates have included:

1. Recognizing and enforcing existing laws and rules regarding the provision of accommodations to Deaf inmates.
2. Appropriate funding to provide accommodations for Deaf inmates.
3. Identifying inmates who are Deaf through screening.
4. Creating separate units within correctional facilities for Deaf inmates.
5. Training for correctional administration, officers, and staff on the needs and accommodations for Deaf inmates.

4.8 Correctional Facilities and Compliance with Accommodations

In 2017, Florida Department of Corrections recognized that they were not in compliance with providing inmates with interpreters during medical appointments and disciplinary hearings (Disability Rights Florida, Inc., v. Jones, 2017), and a similar settlement in South Carolina also outlines the requirements for auxiliary aids, which included ASL interpreters (Settlement Between the United States of America and South Carolina Department of Corrections Under the Americans with Disabilities Act, 2018). In Heyer v. U.S. Bureau of Prisons (2017), it was shown that Heyer, a deaf man, was not provided with an ASL interpreter despite the prison being aware that he was deaf, Heyer's multiple requests for an interpreter based on his need for effective communication for medical treatment. The Fourth Circuit Court of Appeals found that the Bureau of Prisons' failure to provide interpreters violated Heyer's fifth Amendment rights and was constituted "deliberate indifference" (Heyer v. US Bureau of Prisons, 2017).

4.9 Conclusion

Just like in other legal situations, correctional systems pose a challenge for both the Deaf inmate and staff. Training correctional administrators, officers, and other staff on the requirements of providing accommodations, obtaining accommodations, and providing accommodations to the Deaf inmate is an important consideration. Deaf inmates face unique difficulties because of their hearing loss and communication abilities, and this may predispose them or increase the risk of victimization and isolation. Correctional staff should be aware of these issues and screen for Deaf inmates in order to provide accommodations and to be observant of any difficulties the Deaf inmate may be experiencing while incarcerated.

References

Ballinger, J., & Nguyen, V. (2019). *Americans with disabilities act: Disability related access for inmates guide*. Southwest ADA Center.

Crewe, B. (2009). *The prisoner society: Power, adaptation and social life in an English prison*. OUP/Clarendon.

Ezekiel, J. (1994). Going from streets, to shelters, to jails. *IRE Journal*, pp 6–7.

Feldman, D. M. (2017). Deaf inmates. In K. R. Kerley (Ed.), *The encyclopedia of corrections*. https://doi.org/10.1002/9781118845387.wbeoc241.

Geer, S. S. (2003). When "equal" means "unequal"—And other legal conundrums for the deaf community. In C. Lucas (Ed.), *Lan-guage and the law in deaf communities* (pp. 82–167). Gallaudet University Press.

Gibbs, A., & Ackerman, N. (1999). Deaf prisoners. *Prison Service Journal, 122*(52), 31–32.

Goben, B., Enos, K., & Andrews, J. (2009). *What to do? In jail but can't read the inmate handbook: Solutions for the deaf offender*. Unpublished manuscript, Lamar University.

Grossman, L. P. (2015). A prison within a prison: The deaf inmate. *American Jails, 29*(1), 15–22.

Jeanne, N. (2013, March 28). *Solitary confinement: Mental illness and isolation, healthyplace*. Retrieved on January 14, 2023, from https://www.healthyplace.com/blogs/recoveringfrommentalillness/2013/03/solitary-confinement-mental-illness-and-isolation

Justice Department Reaches Agreement with the South Carolina Department of Corrections to Provide Effective Communication to Inmates with Hearing Disabilities. (2018). *Settlement agreement between the United States of America and South Carolina Department of Corrections under the Americans with disabilities act*. Office of Public Affairs, USDOJ, DJ 204-67-174.

Kelly, M. (2017). Sounding out d/deafness: The experiences of d/deaf prisoners. *Journal of Criminal Psychology, 8*(1), 22–32.

Lewis, T. (2014). #DeafInPrison Campaign Fact Sheet 1, 26 June, HERD, www.behearddc.org/images/pdf/deafinprison%20fact%20sheet%20.pdf. Accessed 26 June 2018.

Maruschak, L., Bronson, J., Alper, M. (2021). Disabilities reported by prisoners: survey of prison inmates. Bureau of Justice Statistics. NCJ 252642

McEntee, M. (1993). Mental health and crisis intervention availability for the deaf. *American Annals fo the Deaf, 138*(1), 26–30.

Miller, K. (2001). *Forensic issues of deaf offenders*. Unpublished dissertation. Lamar University.

Miller, K. R. (2002). Population management strategies for deaf and hard-of-hearing offenders. *Corrections Today, 64*(7), 90.

Miller, K. (2004). Linguistic diversity in a Deaf prison population: Implications for due process. *Journal of Deaf Studies and Deaf Education, 9*(1), 112–119.

Miller, K. R., & Vernon, M. (2001). Linguistic diversity in deaf defendants and due process. *Journal of Deaf Studies and Deaf Education, 6*(3), 226–234.

Miller, K. R., Vernon, M., & Capela, N. (2005). Violent offenders in a deaf prison population. *Journal of Deaf Studies and Deaf Education, 10*(4), 417–425.

Musumerci, M. B. (2006). Confronting sentences that silence: The Americans with disabilities act's effective communications man-date for prisoners and probationers who are deaf. *Journal of Poverty Law and Policy, 39*(11), 627–638.

Novic, S. (2018, June 21). Deaf prisoners are trapped in frightening isolation. *CNN*. https://edition.cnn.com/2018/06/21/opinions/aclu-georgia-deaf-abuse-lawsuit-novic/index.html

Ridgeway, J. (2012). The silent treatment. *Mother Jones, 37*(2), 56–59.

Tucker, B. P. (1988). Deaf prison prisoners: A time to be heard. *Loyola of Los Angeles Law Review, 22*, 1–71.

Vernon, M. (2009). ADA routinely violated by prisons in the case of deaf prisoners. *Prison Legal News, 20*(7), 14–15.

Vernon, M. (2010). The horror of being deaf and in prison. *American Annals of the Deaf, 155*(3), 311–321.

Vernon, M., & Leigh, I. W. (2007). Mental health services for people who are deaf. *American Annals of the Deaf, 152*(4), 374–381.

Vernon, M., & Miller, K. (2005). Obstacles faced by deaf people in the criminal justice system. *American Annals of the Deaf, 150*(3), 283–291.

Index

D. M. Feldman et al., *Intersections of the Legal System and the Deaf Community*, SpringerBriefs in Psychology, https://doi.org/10.1007/978-3-031-28100-6

www.ingramcontent.com/pod-product-compliance
Ingram Content Group UK Ltd.
Pitfield, Milton Keynes, MK11 3LW, UK
UKHW020152290926
15471UKWH00004B/821
9783031280993